Shanghai 2020

Kerry Brown

FOREIGN LANGUAGES PRESS

First Edition 2013

Publishers:
China International Publishing Group
Information Office of Shanghai Municipality

ISBN 978-7-119-08630-9
© Foreign Languages Press Co. Ltd, Beijing, China, 2013
Published by Foreign Languages Press Co. Ltd
24 Baiwanzhuang Road, Beijing 100037, China
http://www.flp.com.cn E-mail: flp@cipg.org.cn
Distributed by China International Book Trading Corporation
35 Chegongzhuang Xilu, Beijing 100044, China
P.O. Box 399, Beijing, China
Printed in the People's Republic of China

Contents

Introduction ... 1
Shanghai Chronology ... 14

Chapter One
The History and Future of the City ... 24
Shanghai Through the Bund ... 25
The Future in the Past ... 34

Chapter Two
The Opening Up of the City from 1990 ... 38
Special Economic Zones ... 40
Urban Planning and the Development of the City ... 42
Pudong ... 45
The Shanghai Stock Exchange ... 52
Planning the Future: The 2001 Master Plan ... 54
Shanghai and the Five Year Plans ... 59
Shanghai's Own Programme 2011-2015 ... 64
The Key Areas of the 12th Five Year Programme ... 66
Internationalisation ... 71
Conclusion ... 75

■ Chapter Three
  Shanghai and Globalisation: The 2010 Expo   78
  Expos in General   82
  The World in One City for Six Months   84
  Expo Assessment   87
  The Sustainable Use of the Expo Site   90
  What Is Worth It?   93
  Shanghai Disneyland   94
  International Events   96
  The Expo, International Events and the Meaning of the
  Shanghai's Internationalisation   97

■ Chapter Four
  Shanghai Society and Governance   100
  Administrative Structures   102
  A Migrant City?   107
  The Core Issue: Inequality   110
  Governing Shanghai at the Grassroots   111
  Education   116
  Healthcare   120
  Social Welfare   124
  The Role of International Migration and Citizens 125
  Shanghai 2020: The Creation of a Middle Class Society 128

Chapter Five
The Shanghai Economy — 132
- The Phases of Development — 134
- The Impact of Entry to the World Trade Organisation 2001 — 140
- The Role of International Trade: Imports and Exports — 143
- Agriculture — 147
- IT — 148
- Property — 148
- Foreign Direct Investment in Shanghai — 150
- Shanghai Outward Investment — 158
- China (Shanghai) Pilot Free Trade Zone — 160
- Shanghai Economy 2020 — 167

Chapter Six
Shanghai as an International Finance Centre — 174
- A Brief History — 175
- Development of the Finance Sector — 179
- The Vision for the City's Financial Service — 181
- The Development of Shanghai as an International Finance Centre – the Products — 184
- A Tale of Two International Banks in Shanghai — 190
- Internationalisation of the RMB — 191
- Challenges for the Future — 194

Chapter Seven
Shanghai's Environment — 198
China's National Environmental Challenges: Context — 200
Shanghai's Natural Environment — 201
Shanghai Energy — 204
The Regeneration of the City — 205
The New Built Environment — 209
Food Security — 211
Sustainability and the Environment: The Bigger Picture — 213

Chapter Eight
Shanghai Culture — 218
Soft Power — 221
The Culture of a City of Wellbeing — 225
What Does It Mean to Be Shanghainese? — 226
Cultural Innovation — 228
The Shanghai Brand — 229

Conclusion — 232
Shanghai 2020 — 233

The Local Dimension	234
Shanghai's Future in the National Context	238
Shanghai in the Global Context	242
What Do the Shanghainese Want?	247

Bibliography 252

Acknowledgements 256

Introduction

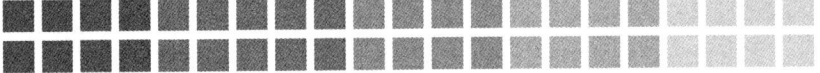

This is a book about one of the most dynamic, fastest growing cities on earth. It is about a city in a country which is engaging with modernity in ways which have utterly reshaped its economy and society since the start of the reform and opening up process more than three decades ago in 1978. It is about how a place is returning to its historic role as a great crossing point, a window from the world onto China and China onto the world. It is about somewhere where the East meets West, but where the East also meets itself. This is finally the personal story of engagement with the great ambitions of this city, albeit for only a tiny moment of this great story as it unfolds.

Shanghai has been one of the crucibles of Chinese modernity since the end of the 19th century. It grew famous as a place of fashion and excess in the 1920s and 1930s, with figures as disparate as Albert Einstein and Charles Chaplin visiting. It was a place of refuge for Jewish people who managed to arrive there in the Second World War, and became, in those devastating years, one of the battlefronts in the epic fight for national integrity against the Japanese. It was the city in which the first ever Congress of the Communist Party of China was held in 1921, but also the place the Party activists were brutally exiled from in 1927 when the Nationalists undertook a bloody purge. It was this city that Mao Zedong came to, throughout his period as Chairman of the Party from 1949 to 1976, and it was in this city that the most radical activists of the Cultural Revolution found their base.

Those who come to Shanghai today for the first time have to hold this extraordinary history, with its rich and complex movements and countercurrents, alongside the physical impression of a place which has literally rebuilt and renovated itself in three decades. If any landscape of modern China symbolizes the striving of the whole country around it and its aspirations, it is the skyline of Pudong south of the Huangpu river, seen from beside the historic buildings along the Bund in the north which were constructed in one era of redefinition and rediscovery and are now being remade and renovated for another (this will be described in the first chapter). By the grand old Custom House, once more the headquarters of a bank, visitors can look across over the waters of the river pulsing with goods and passenger ships, to the vast array of skyscrapers the other side. Until 1990, this area was the home of run down warehouses, derelict land, and some agricultural small holdings. But in that year, as this book will explain, the historic decision was made to grant Shanghai the same status as a special economic zone that had seen places like Shenzhen grow from fishing towns of a few tens of thousands of people to cities of over ten million inhabitants.

Making Shanghai a special zone gave the green light to land development, to special policies that allowed the manufacture of goods for export, and to engaging with new processes of economic activity globally which, within a decade, transformed the city physically and socially. By the year in which China entered the World Trade Organisation (WTO), in 2001, Pudong had changed beyond recognition. It had the world's tallest hotel, and some of its biggest skyscrapers, one of which was under construction and which would become, briefly, the world's tallest building. Elsewhere in the city, a deepwater port was being constructed, carrying the city towards fulfilling the aspiration of becoming the world's busiest freight port – an objective that was achieved in 2010. In Lujiazui, the city had constructed a financial district, attracting banks, insurance companies, and multinationals to set up representative offices and joint ventures.

Delegations from around the world, many from the 64 cities with which Shanghai had twinned, came to marvel at this new city being constructed, its population swelling by half a million people a year, as it exploded forward 23 million people by 2012. All of this culminated in the Shanghai Expo held in 2010, an event which saw over 70 million people visit.

Shanghai is a city which is uniquely embracing the challenge of the future. It is doing this through rearticulating its identity as these dynamic changes occur around it, rebranding itself in ways which link its history as a place distinctly Chinese but also international with a vision of what a major city should be in the twenty-first century in the midst of almost constant change. It is a city which links the local with the global in ways which have interest and resonance for other places that also aspire to globalise while maintaining their distinctive character. It is a city therefore which, while learning, also now has much to teach others. This theme of a city constantly on the move but always trying to catch up with itself as it moves swiftly ahead, will return throughout this book.

In trying to understand what is happening in Shanghai and how things might develop in the future is, in many ways, also trying to understand the complexities, ambiguities and challenges facing modern China as it continues along the path of reaching middle income country status by 2020. In per capita terms, Shanghai has already arrived where other places within the country need to go. Its per capita levels of wealth stand in 2012 above ten thousand USD, more than double the national average. It has one of the best healthcare systems, some of the best universities, some of the most innovative companies, and an economy that is quickly moving towards service industry rather than manufacturing. Those that come to the Bund to gaze over the modern skyline of the city often feel like they are looking not just at the present, but at the future, and at what the rest of the country wishes to become in a few years.

This is necessarily a personal account as much as it is a book about a city. Shanghai belongs to anyone who visits the city, and within it they create narratives of engagement, and links between their own lives and the immense project of the city itself as it moves into the future, carrying aspirations but also fears. I first visited the city as an official from the British government in 1998, fresh from London and working in the Foreign Office. I remember the ways in which, during the evening as people were returning home, Nanjing Street was so clogged with bicycle traffic it was hard to get across the road to the other side. The Bund at that time was only half renovated. There were large areas of the city that were still being replanned. The only airport was the old fashioned and greatly overused Hongqiao. The city's roadwork system was at capacity. Only a couple of metro lines existed.

As a diplomat based in Beijing I had to come to Shanghai often between 2000 and 2003. It was an inevitable part of any VIP itinerary to the country. Dignitaries were taken to look at Pudong, to visit companies which had located in the city, one of the most successful at that time being B&Q, a retailer dealing in household goods which was taking advantage of the boom in house ownership. British companies, along with other European and American ones, flocked to the city, setting up offices, trying to break into the vast Chinese market they were hoping to find spread around them. Every time I visited, I saw more new luxurious hotels spring up. My own favourite, however, remained the old Astor House Hotel, one of the survivors of the late 19th century, sitting in a relatively secluded spot opposite the large Russian consulate by Suzhou River and just along from the Bund. The Astor House hotel underwent extensive renovations in the mid 2000s, and its cool, quiet rooms were places of refuge from the high levels of energy elsewhere in the city. Some of them had the same wooden floors, and the same ambience that must have existed when Premier Zhou Enlai stayed in the hotel before 1949. The old dining hall beyond the dark wooded entry lobby remains a popular place for weddings to this day.

From 2006 to 2010, I was a frequent visitor to the city, and grew far more familiar with it, through working as advisor to the British city twinned with Shanghai, Liverpool. Liverpool had historic links with Shanghai, and some similarities in terms of its economy and function. It was a port city that had grown wealthy through an explosion of global trade in the late 19th and early 20th century. Like Shanghai, its history had given it a rich legacy of historic buildings put up during this phase of prosperity. Like Shanghai, it had gone through a period of quietness, in which trade had declined and the stock of older buildings fallen into disrepair. And like Shanghai, it was undertaking a new era of renovation and rediscovery of its heritage. There were more specific links. Liverpool is the home of the oldest Chinese community in Europe, from the middle of the 19th century. Many of those who had come to settle in the city were sailors, who had originated from Shanghai. This was formally recognized in 1999 when the two cities signed a twinning arrangement. A Liverpool Shanghai Partnership was subsequently set up, which I ran for four years, and Liverpool, as the culmination of this took a stand at the Shanghai Expo in the Urban Regeneration city area in 2010.

What made the cities different however was simply the scale at which they were doing things. Liverpool had experienced depopulation in the 1960s, as the shipping industry declined and freight traffic went elsewhere. From 700 thousand at its height before the 1940s, the population of the city fell to a little below half a million. For Shanghai, things were different. From the 1970s, its population crept up above ten million, until, by 2012, it had reached 23 million, and was set to be 28 million. Over 12 thousand new people were arriving each week, enough to comfortably create a new Liverpool each year. Shanghai was a city with over 2000 skyscrapers, whereas Liverpool only had a handful. And while Shanghai's ports after the construction of the vast deepwater port in the late 2000s had become the busiest in the world, Liverpool's had stagnated, despite worthy efforts to revitalize the city as a transport hub.

One thing Liverpool did have that resonated with Shanghai's aspirations was a thriving education sector, and a very active regeneration plan. In the areas around the once bereft Albert Docks,

Liverpool had created an exciting and attractive residential and museum zone, with the centerpiece being the Tate Liverpool gallery and the Museum of Slavery. Large parts of the city were redeveloping their remarkable Georgian architecture from a period over 200 years before. The proudest architectural asset of the city were the 'Three Graces,' large buildings sitting on the waterfront, one of which had been the largest concrete construction ever assembled when it had been built in the early 1900s.

Delegations I took to Shanghai from Liverpool often looked at the Bund as somehow being derivative of these buildings. This was based more on emotion than logic. In fact, as this book will show in its chapter on the history of the city, many of the structures that now sit along the Bund predate the Three Graces in Liverpool by many decades. But they belong to a common tradition of international colonial style architecture, and have authentic common links from European schools of architecture. In that sense, they are both great testaments to an earlier period of globalization during one of the most dynamic phases of industrialization and the creation of the modern capitalist economy. There, at least, they can be seen as monuments with a shared root.

The challenge of how Shanghai seeks to respect and stand by its historic roots as a place in which there are some of the world's best and most innovative early industrial buildings and modernist monuments, while also moving towards a future in which there will be enormous pressures on its environment and on the very sustainability of the city is one that will reoccur throughout this book. In many ways, Shanghai's challenge is similar to that of many other cities. It will continue to be pulled on the one hand between moving into a future in which lifestyles and economic trends are very different to that of even the recent past while on the other hand trying to preserve the material remnants of an earlier period and supply some sense of stability and continuity between the two. How does Shanghai fulfill this responsibility of both preserving but also transforming? How does it modernize, but remain true to its historic

Introduction

roots? This is a fundamental question which will be addressed, in many different sections of this book. These questions are particularly powerful because the impulses of change and modernity in Shanghai are currently perhaps more extreme in degree and scale than any other place in the world. Solving the problems of combining respect for what has been left from the past but also how to create a new city in Shanghai will offer lessons for elsewhere. We can see this as perhaps the fundamental challenge of the city as it moves more deeply into the 21st century.

Shanghai fascinates everyone particularly because it seems to encapsulate the mood and spirit of the whole of China as it continues its grand experiment in reform and change. It's a city that carries meaning and evokes strong responses not just from foreigners, but also from Chinese. In the words of one long term resident of Shanghai originally from the UK interviewed for this book, this is a place not only where 'east meets west' but also where 'east meets east.'[1] The city physically embodies the dynamism of China's vision of modernity, and the vivid impact this has on people when they first encounter the new and evolving skyline of Pudong is memorable. In 2012 alone, in two major Hollywood films, *Skyfall*, the latest in the 007 James Bond series and *Looper*, key scenes were set in Shanghai. In the first, Bond tracks down an assassin linked to a global criminal who has come to Shanghai to execute a target in one of the floors of an immense new skyscraper in the city centre. In *Looper*, the character played by Bruce Willis finds himself in the city thirty years from today, a telling indication of how, in much popular western imagination, Shanghai is linked to futurism rather than just modernity. The city's attributes in this film of flashing neon lights and powerful modern skyscraper architecture however are very similar to what a visitor would find already exist in the real city today.

The American based economist Yasheng Huang in his *Capitalism with Chinese Characteristics* states that 'Nowhere else in the world

---

1. Interview, Shanghai, November 2012

7

has Shanghai inspired more imagination – and despair – than the Indian city of Mumbai...' Indian intellectuals and business people ask, often in great exasperation, 'Why cannot Mumbai be more like Shanghai?' [2] Huang refers to the famous journey that visitors take from the Pudong International Airport along the Maglev railway travelling at speeds up to 450 km an hour into the city. 'Much of the admiration for Shanghai,' he states, 'is based on visual evidence.' [3] That evidence is often seductive and detracts from the more complex human and social story that is wrapped up in the buildings and infrastructure that lies before people when they look at the city, wherever they come from.

The Geography and Climate of Shanghai

Shanghai is located on the West coast of the Pacific Ocean and the central section of the north-south coastline of China, bordering Jiangsu Province and Zhejiang Province to the West. It covers 6,219 square kilometers, with a water area of 122 square kilometers, and the whole municipal region also includes Chongming Island, the third largest in China with an area of 1,041 square kilometers. For the total area of Shanghai, 3,924 square kilometers are defined as urban, and 2,416 as rural.

The city has a humid subtropical climate, with four seasons ranging from 1 degree Celsius (35 Fahrenheit) in January to 31 degrees Celsius (90 degrees Fahrenheit) in July.

---

2. Yasheng Huang. *Capitalism with Chinese Characteristics: Entrepreneurship and the State.* Cambridge University Press, Cambridge, 2008, p.175.
3. Ibid., p.176.

Introduction

The breathless speed at which the Chinese economy has grown over the last three decades since reform and opening up started in the late 1970s can best be captured by 'Great Leap Forward', a book produced under the architect Rem Koolhaas and a team around him in 2001. While this work is not so much about Shanghai, but two other cities – Shenzhen, where an explosion of building and development occurred after it was designated as a Special Economic Zone in 1980, and Zhuhai, which was accorded similar status in 1984 – generically it captures well the energy and force of reform as it gathers momentum in modern China. For both of these cities, communities grew massively as migrants came in to take up the new jobs being created in the manufacturing. Shenzhen at some points in the 1980s had a growth rate of over 40 per cent a year. In Zhuhai, the book offers a pictorial and written essay on the plans that the city had in 2001 for its greater development, with roads, skyrise buildings, factories, entertainment centres, ports all listed from government plans. The impact of reading this even today ten years later underlines the sheer ambition and the scale at which some parts of China are attempting to embrace modernity.[4] In many ways, Shanghai now takes the lead in this ambitiousness. The kinds of vision and ambition that the book captures has congregated in the city, making it a place people increasingly talk about as the best to look when you wish to find the way the rest of China might go in a few years time.

Julia Lovell testifies to the challenges of trying to conceptualise and keep up with the speed of this change and its human impact in her brief work on modernism in Chinese architecture, 'Splendidly Fantastic'. In this she states that 'the Chinese have invested more meaning in the built environment than any other civilization.' For Shenzhen, she noted that the way in which the city had exploded architecturally had 'humiliated vision'. For Pudong, it is China's 'first

---

4. Rem Koolhaas; Jeffrey Inaba; Sze Tsung Leong; Chuihua Judy Chung (eds). *Great Leap Forward*. Taschen, Cologne, 2001.

9

global architectural mega project.'[5] All of this received the ultimate celebrity accolade when US heiress and celebrity Paris Hilton visited the city in 2007, and declared that she thought the city 'looks like the future'.[6] The ways in which the city encapsulates aspiration, futurism and modernity physically are precisely the things that attract commentators.

For all of this epic and dramatic change, much of which is unprecedented in human history, at the heart of the story of modern China, and of Shanghai, and the transformation it is undergoing, is that of its people. It is their energy, their hard work, and their aspirations that are building the future, and shaping the kind of country China is now becoming. Bringing the story of the city's development down to this human level therefore will be an important challenge in this work. While understanding the grand trends that are taking place is of course important, as much as possible this book tries to look at things from within the city, from the eyes of those intimately involved with its current and future planning, either as officials, as business people, citizens, or residents. Capturing the human face of Shanghai, and seeing how it represents the rest of China, is important, rather than being overwhelmed by the scale and velocity of change that is happening.

The plan of this book is very simple. In the first chapter, I will look at the history of the City, and of its origins back over seven centuries, to the period of its first internationalization in the 1930s. I will aim to encapsulate this history simply through the stories of the main buildings now famously ranged along the Bund, the world famous historic site which faces the river running west to east to where the Suzhou River interrupts the bay line. Through the tale each of these buildings hold, I will try to describe the narrative of history by which the city has grown and developed, hoping to offer in this way

---

5. Julia Lovell. *Splendidly Fantastic: Architecture and Power Games in China*. Streika Press, Amazon and IBookstores, 2012
6. Cited at http://www.people.com/people/article/0,,20162187,00.html, accessed 9 December, 2012

an easily graspable route to understanding the different phases of Shanghai's modern growth and how these relate to its vision for the future.

In the second chapter, I will move on to the period of real renaissance for Shanghai as a modern commercial and financial centre in 1990 when it was declared one of the Special Economic Zones. I will place this announcement in the context of China's opening up and internationalisation through the previous decade, and then address both how the city was developed from 1990s, where the key growth strategies were, the creation of a stock market in the city, and the current Five Year Programme and the 2002 City Plan and what impact these had, and are having.

In the third chapter, I will concentrate on the Shanghai 2010 Expo, a major event which saw the city after two decades of reforming and opening up showcase itself to the world, and to people from other parts of China. The Expo, like the Beijing Olympics of two years before, saw the development of major infrastructure projects but also the unprecedented accommodation of over 70 million visitors in a six month period while the event was being held. Through the story of the planning, running and the legacy of the Expo, I will look at what lessons were learned from this vast public event, where it has taken the city's strategy, and what impact it is likely to have on the city's future.

In the fourth chapter, I will look at the society of Shanghai, a microcosm of all the dynamic change that is happening elsewhere in the country, and an area in which immense and very unpredictable events are happening. Shanghai will increase its population by over 5 million in the decade up to 2022, coming to an area a little more than 650 square kilometers. This will pose questions about the governance of the city and to social cohesion within it. I will look at infrastructure of government in the city, from the municipal level down to household committees, the impact of rapid development on lifestyles and on the expectations of modern Shanghai people, and where their society might be developing in the coming decade. In particular, I will look at profiles of eminent people in the city to see what they tell us about the spirit of the city and the real stories of people who live there. I will finally look at how with these challenges the city will be sustainable in terms of governance and cohesion in the coming decade.

In the fifth chapter, I will look at the economy of the city in the last five years, focusing particularly on key sectors like finance and hi-tech. In particular, I will present case studies of two key companies who have come from abroad to operate in the city, and two who are local companies now looking to globalize. I will then look at the key ecomomic challenges for the city in the coming decade, based on its current plans, and how it wishes to transform to a more service sector orientated economic model. I will then propose how the city might overcome these as it travels towards a middle income city with double the per capita GDP of today.

In the sixth chapter, I will concentrate on the financial services sector, showing how the city is trying to create an internationally competitive banking, investment and insurance hub, but one which can operate as the interface between the rest of China and the world. I will in particular concentrate on the regulatory, human capital and business challenges that derive from this, and project how Shanghai might places itself beside Hong Kong, London, Tokyo and New York as a place to list, raise capital and invest in the coming decade.

In the seventh chapter I will look at the critical issue of the environment, and the sustainability of the city's development. Like elsewhere in China and the developing world, the impact of modernization on the natural world has been heavy. In Shanghai, a city which has been built on marshland is uniquely vulnerable to rising sea levels and to extreme weather events, which may be the outcome of carbon emission impacts on meteorological patterns. I will look at the ways in which, in projects like Xintiandi, the city has supported regeneration, and how it is aiming to create a sustainable urban model. I will also look at the challenges, and proposals to deal with those, both for those in the city and outside, as it increases its economic importance.

In the eighth chapter I will look at the culture of the city, in terms of its food, and restaurant sectors, its diversity, the ways in which the city aspires to develop soft power in the coming decades, and what issues there might be about spiritual or religious values as the society grows more complex and varied.

I will then offer a conclusion, mapping out Shanghai's key developmental challenges in the next decade against the generic challenges that the country faces as a whole in the important 'China 2030' report issued by the National Development and Reform Commission and the World Bank in 2012. I will in particular place voices of those I have interviewed from their different sectors and backgrounds into this chapter, showing how they as individuals see the city in a decade's time.

Because this is a book about Shanghai's future, the present and the past are important as indicators of where the city should be going. I have located this vision for the city very much within the vision that China has for itself, as a harmonious, middle income, creative society by the next decade. But in many ways, Shanghai is placed to reach this benchmark much earlier than elsewhere in the country, showing the rest of the country what it looks like. For this reason, this book has been written also from a very practical perspective – as offering ideas in different areas to how the city, through relying on its own resources and through international cooperation, might be able to achieve its objectives in the following decade. In many ways, as I will seek to argue, Shanghai's future is also our future, wherever we are and for that reason should be something in which we are all engaged and involved.

Shanghai Chronology

Around 6,000 years ago	Sites around Shanghai dating back to the Neolithic Period indicate that the west part of today's Shanghai had become land more than 6,000 years ago and there where people living in the area at that time. Those ancestors first lived by hunting, fishing and grazing and later by farming.
751 (Tianbao Years of Tang Danasty)	Huating County, located in a swampy area east of Suzhou, was established in today's Songjiang District with 12,780 households.
1278	During the Yuan Dynasty (1271-1368), Huating County was renamed to SongJiang County in 1278.
1292	Shanghai County was officially set up in today's Minhang District with households of more than 72,500, under the jurisdiction of Huating County.
Ming Dynasty (1368-1644)	By the Ming Dynasty, Shanghai has already grown into the largest cotton spinning base in China. Its textiles were popular at home and abroad.
1645	The army of the Qing took over the city after three massacres and attacks of the city.

Introduction

1685	In 1685 during the Qing Dynasty (1644 - 1911), the Customs Office was established in the city. Consequently unprecedented progress was made in the shipping industry including freshwater carriage, Yangtze River shipping, coastal liners and international shipping. The port of Shanghai came to handle the largest quantities of imported and exported cotton cloth. Many ships berthed in the port, making it the main transfer point of maritime trade. As time passed, Shanghai gained its position as an important economic power, a water transport center and an international trading port in China.
1832 (during the Qing Dynasty 1644-1911)	The officials from the British East India Company began to explore Shanghai in 1832 for the purpose of trading in tea, silk and opium. They arrived with the cruise of Amherst (named after Lord Amherst) and ported at Shanghai for 18 days.
1842	In 1842, the British Navy led by the General, William Parker, intruded into Shanghai on 19 June and the city was temporarily held by British forces.
29 Aug.	The war ended with the "Treaty of Nanjing". Representatives from both sides signed the treaty on 29 Aug., which opened five treaty ports including Shanghai to international trade.

15

1843 17 Nov.	Shanghai was officially announced for its opening for international trade. George Balfour, the first British consul in Shanghai, started to negotiate with local Shanghai officials on the British settlement in Shanghai.
1845 29 Nov.	The 'Shanghai Land Regulation' was introduced on 29 Nov. and it was followed by the establishment of British concession.
1848 25 Jan.	The French Consul at Shanghai, L.C.N Maximilien Montigry arrived in Shanghai.
March	Anti-Christian Case in Qingpu broke out in 1848 when the Qing Dynasty implemented the second sea transport of Tribute Grain.
27 Nov.	British Consul signed an agreement with Shanghai officials to allow the first expansion of British settlement. The same year, American missionary bishop, William Jones Boone also requested to sign land-deal with Shanghai and was approved to build the American concession in Hongkou district.
1849	Agreement between France and Shanghai was signed on 6 April. France then established its own French concession under French consular jurisdiction.
1853	The 'Small Sword Society' led by Liu Lichuan took over the town hall and set up a command post at Yiyuan on 7 Sep.

Introduction

1860 Aug.	Taiping troop attempted to take Shanghai in Aug. but was repulsed by the force of British army based in Shanghai.
1861 29 Oct.	The first expansion of French concession, as wide as nearly 130 acreages.
1862	The second attempt of Taiping rebels to take Shanghai in Jan. Taiping rebels' third attempt to take Shanghai in May.
1865	The British HSBC established its Shanghai branch and started its operation on 3 April. General Bureau of Machine Manufacture of Jiangnan was established on 29 Sep.
1867	Shanghai Fire Bridge was established by the Shanghai Municipal Council on 7 Jan. By the late-1860s Shanghai's official governing body had been practically transferred from the individual concessions to the Shanghai Municipal Council（工部局）
1872	*Declaration* (*Shun Pao*, a Chinese Newspaper) was founded by the British merchant Ernst Major on 30 April. The first group of 30 Chinese students boarded the cruise in Shanghai and headed for America for studying abroad on 11 Aug.

17

1876	The first railroad in China, the Sunghu railway, began service in July and extended to Woosung road in Dec. It was built by British company Jardine & Matheson without permission of Qing government, and purchased by Qing viceroy Shen Baozhen and dismantled in mid Dec.
1884	*Dianshizhai Huabao*, one of the most significant pictorials in late-Qing China was launched by Englishman Ernst Major on 8 May.
1894 1 Aug.	War of Jiawu (The First Sino-Japanese War) occurred. The American Consul declared to take over Japan's Consulate in Shanghai and relevant business.
1895 Mid of Nov.	Kang Youwei, Chinese scholar, prominent political thinker and reformer of the late-Qing Dynasty, launched the Qiangxuehui (Society for National Strengthening) in Shanghai.
1896	Nanyang Public School was founded in Shanghai on 8 April by Sheng Xuanhuai who proposed the idea to Guangxu Emperor and has become the first President of the first University in Shanghai, now known as Shanghai Jiaotong University.
9 Aug.	*Shanghai Shiwu Bao* was launched by Liang Qichao, who proposed the Wuxu Reform (Hundred Days' Reform) to Emperor Guangxu (reigned 1871-1908) together with Kang Youwei.

11 Aug.	Motion pictures were introduced to China in 1896 and the first recorded screening of a motion picture occurred in Shanghai.
Oct.	*The Su Pao*, a daily newspaper founded by Hu Zhang, first appeared in Shanghai.
9 Nov.	The Qing government assigned Sheng Xuanhuai to take charge of the Songhu railway construction project.
1897	The Commercial Press in Shanghai, the first modern publishing organization in China, was founded by Xia Ruifang and Bao Xiangchang in Feb. The Imperial Bank of China, China's first modern bank, was launched on 27 May.
1898	*Female School Newspaper*, the first women's newspaper in China, was launched in Shanghai by female students on 24 July. The construction of Songhu railway was completed on 5 Aug. and the service started on 1 Sep.
1899 8 May	Shanghai International Settlement was formally named after the expansion of British and American settlements.
1900 26 Jan.	Jiang Yuansan, the General officer of Shanghai Cable & Wireless, coordinated with 1,231 people in Shanghai to present the request asking Emperor Guangxu to step down. Qing government declared the war against those 8 countries on 26 June.

1901 15 Mar.	More than 200 people assembled in Zhangyuan against the Russia, later on 24 Zhangyuan gathered nearly 1,000 people in Shanghai fighting for the same request.
1911	Republic of China was established after the Xinhai Revolution which ended China's last imperial Qing dynasty. Shanghai was taken over on 6 Nov. Chen Qimei was appointed the first military governor of Shanghai. Shanghai has become the focal points of major activities which would weigh heavily in shaping modern China.
1919 10 Oct.	Dr. Sun Yat-sen resurrected the KMT in 1919 under the name of Chinese Kuomintang and headquartered in Shanghai (It was restored to Guangdong in 1920).
1921	The first CPC Party Congress was held in Shanghai on 23 July.
1925 1927	Shanghai was made a special municipality in 1925 and the government of Shanghai municipality was established in 1927. Huang Fu was the first mayor of Shanghai (July 1929-April 1929).
1930	Shanghai was renamed to Shanghai Municipality on 1 July.

Introduction

1932	The Japanese Navy bombed Shanghai on 28 Jan, nominally to crush Chinese students protest against the Japanese occupation of Manchuria (known in China as the January 28 Incident).
1937	Battle of Shanghai (known in China as the Battle of Songhu). Shanghai fell after the Battle of Shanghai and remained occupied by Japan until the surrender of Japan in 1945. Under Japanese rule, the foreign concessions remained intact until December 1941.
1949	On 27 May, Shanghai came under Communist control.
1964	The Pakistan International Airlines started flying to Shanghai on 29 April (PIA was the first non-communist airline flying to PRC).
1967	Shanghai People's Commune (上海人民公社) was established during China's Culture Revolution (1966-1976) in early 1967.
1972	US President Richard Nixon visited China (PRC) during Feb. 21–28. The visit marked the first visit of a US President to PRC and ended 25 years of separation between the two sides (He had visited Beijing, Shanghai and Hangzhou during his short visit).

1980	More than 400,000 educated youths who were sent to live and work in agrarian areas during the Down to the Countryside Movement had eventually returned and received relocation.
1990	The Central Government and State Council approved the Pudong development plan.
1993	The central government decided to set up a Special Economic Zone in Chuansha, creating Pudong New Area. The western tip of the Pudong district was designed as the Lujiazui Finance and Trade Zone and was proposed to become the new financial centre of modern China.
1994	The Lanyin Hukou (Blue Hukou) was introduced by the city government to welcome skilled and qualified migrants by issuing them the blue hukou card (which was replaced by a full residence permit (*juzhuzheng*) in 2002).
1995	Shanghai Metro's first line was launched in April 1995, making Shanghai the 3rd city in China, after Beijing and Tianjin, to have a rapid transit system.
1996	The New Shanghai Museum and the New Shanghai Library were opened in Oct. and Dec.

Introduction

1998	The Shanghai Grand Theatre was opened in August 27, 1998 with a performance of Swan Lake by the National (Beijing) Ballet Company.
2004	Beginning in 2004, Shanghai started hosting the Chinese Grand Prix, one round of the Formula One World Championship.
2010	World Expo 2010 Shanghai was held on both banks of the Huangpu River in Shanghai from 1 May to 31 Oct. 2010 (Shanghai Expo had the largest number of countries participating and was also the largest World's Fair site ever at 5.28 square km).
2013 29 Sep.	China (Shanghai) Pilot Free Trade Zone was established.

Chapter One

The History and Future of the City

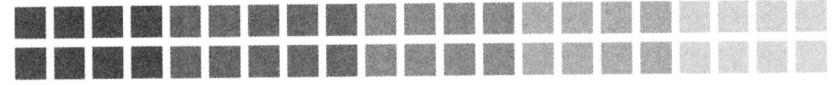

Shanghai Through the Bund

Those who arrive in Shanghai today see a city where much appears to be new, somewhere that has seen many of its streets and districts remade over the last decades. For many of these visitors, the most dramatic scenes are the new skyscrapers in the redeveloped Pudong area, on the site of what were once warehouses and which now constitute the financial district. Here they can stare upon record breaking structures, from the world's tallest hotel, to a building which a few years ago was briefly the highest on the planet. But these visitors can also find plenty of survivors from a previous era of bold modernizing. Shanghai is not a newcomer to modernity. Right at the heart of the city, walking along the Bund at the side of the great Huangpu River running west to east through the centre of the city, they will find one of the world's great monuments from a previous era of globalization and modernity, and somewhere that offers a basis on which to build the present and future aspirations of the city to be a major finance and commerce centre. These venerable structures counterbalance the swathe of more recent buildings opposite. Standing on the Bund promenade, recently renovated for the Shanghai Expo, one can look partially at the older buildings on the northern side, and then, in the same moment, look across at the newness in the south. This combination of the past, the present, and, to some degree, the future, in one moment is very typical of the image that Shanghai manages to convey.

For all its vibrant and unapologetic modernity, it is the Pudong area, at the base of the Oriental Pearl Radio and Television Tower, built from 1990 to 1994, that one can find a place to start making sense of the past and the present and the relationship between them — the Shanghai History Museum. In this museum, it is the context and development of the city before and during the building of the Bund opposite that is at the forefront. Street scenes from various periods of the city's past are laid out, with life sized reconstructions of buildings, detailing what the city might have looked like over the centuries before. The earliest of these portrays a simple fishing village from seven centuries before, during the Yuan Period (1271-1368). For many, it comes as a big surprise that Shanghai has such an ancient history.

When did Shanghai begin to be a place with a settled sense of its identity? US academic Jeffrey Wasserstrom points out in his study of Shanghai's history that one possible point of origin might be the first time the term 'Shanghai' was used in official Yuan government documents, in 1291. It is to this history that many of the scenes in the museum refer, with its growth through the Ming and early Qing dynasties, as a port and a place where transport links crossed. It is this history that links with another, very different history, and the one that is more familiar to outsiders. This is the story of the period from 1840 which is the more frequent point of departure for the start of Shanghai as a global city. Shanghai, as Wasserstrom pointed out, had a population of a quarter of a million people by the 1830s. It figured in a diplomatic accord in 1843 as, along with four other Chinese communities, a 'treaty port', and it was this date that was

---

1. Jeffrey Wasserstrom. *Global Shanghai, 1850-2010*. Routledge, 2009, pp.2-3.

noted in 1893 when Shanghai celebrated its jubilee.[1] Wasserstrom is keen to bridge this divide between on the one hand the idea of a primitive fishing village prior to 1840, and on the other an urban and growing city after that time. For him, 'many historians… have detailed the existence of quintessentially urban phenomenon prior to that time [meaning 1840].' He quotes a British traveler's account of the city in 1830s:

> *'No other town with which I am acquainted possesses such advantages; it is the great gate – the principle entrance in fact – to the Chinese empire… The tide ebbs and flows a great distance inland, this assisting the natives in the transmission of their exports to Shanghai, or their imports to the most distant parts of the country. The port of Shanghai swarms with boats of all sizes…'*[2]

Wasserstrom alerts us to a complex and varied history, one of mixed influences, where prior to 1840 the city was a considerable and important one. Contrary to much Western historiography, it did not suddenly spring into existence in the middle of the 19th century. Much of the earlier phase of the city's development is now lost under the streets, laying perhaps for archaeologists one day to discover. But recapturing something of the physical feel of the global Shanghai which came into existence in the decades after 1840 is a little easier, for some of its greatest monuments stand along the world famous Bund. Each of these tells stories both about the moment of transformation for Shanghai from its existences prior to 1840, to its redevelopment and regeneration to the modern city. In many ways, the Bund even in its present form testifies to previous forms of modernity, but also to the ways in which that modernity can be refreshed, revised and revitalized. This is an important theme throughout this book.

---

2. Ibid., p.4.

Peter Hibbard, a British writer and historian based in Shanghai for over a decade, has written and researched the history of all of the buildings along the Bund, publishing a meticulous account of each surviving structure. As British historian of 19th and 20th century foreign involvement in China Robert Bickers states in the introduction of this work, 'in many ways [the Bund] used to be China's front door, as ship passengers alighted at the customs jetty from abroad and entered China for the first time. ... That foreign-seeming modernity was a source of pride for many.' It was also an icon, a badge through which the city became known to outsiders and through which it defined itself.[3]

Walking along the Bund today offers a chance to reengage with the city's past, and with these complex currents and countercurrents from its previous incarnations. Here the memory traces that these have left both in the buildings and the built environment are authentic and strong. Most people from Europe or North America to this day would associate this view with Shanghai's history and would align it with images they have seen in old photos, films or portrayals in books. For them, these recall the period in the 1930s, when this was a city that accommodated Hollywood film stars, visiting dignitaries and important politicians from across the world. It was this that figured in many Hollywood stories, an exotic and exciting place where the rest of the world came to meet with China.

The Bund still encapsulates this. Walking along the waterfront down east by the side of the river, one is struck by diversity and variety of the buildings. The Bund captures in stone the various narratives of Shanghai as it has developed and engaged and is continuing to engage, with modernity. In many ways it is a living monument to this, to the phases of openness and industrialization over the last century and a half. The buildings here were connected with architects who were mostly from outside China, but who came to the city

---

3. Peter Hibbard. *The Bund: Shanghai*. Odyssey Books, Hong Kong, 2007, p.4.

to practice, bringing with them new styles, and innovating in ways which were unique. The Union Building, the third along the Bund was the first in Shanghai to use full skeletal steel in its framework. Number one the Bund, in what was called the McBain building, had a vast ten thousand square metres floor space when it was built between 1913 and 1915 and was acknowledged after its completion as the grandest building along what was nicknamed at the time the 'billion dollar skyline'. Number seven, the Great Northern Telegraph Company Building, designed by the Atkinson and Dallas practice and opened in 1908, was the first building in China to have a state of the art pneumatic tube system to handle telegrams and have public telephones. The Russo Chinese Bank (now the Shanghai Gold Exchange) at Number 15, dating back to 1902, was designed by German Heinrich Becker who had arrived in the city in 1899 and was the first building in Shanghai to have an elevator, and to be heated with hot air pipes and electric fans and lights.

The Bund monuments also testify to a period of commerce and internationalized trade. The McBain building referred to above housed the British Chamber of Commerce, and was named after a businessman who owned Shanghai's first private aircraft. Number Five, the NKK Building, was commissioned from the architects Lester, Johnston and Morris in neo-renaissance style and completed in 1921. NKK refers to Nisshin Kisen Kaisha, the Japanese fire insurance company. It now houses, amongst other businesses, the Glamour Bar (see below). At Number 9 is the China Merchants Steam Navigation Company Building, home to the first Chinese company to establish itself on the Bund which had the site designed by Atkinson and Dallas and opened in 1901.

Perhaps the greatest building still testifying to this early era of international trade based in the city and its connection to global finance is the Hongkong and Shanghai Bank Building, with its cupola and imposing façade. The Chief Manager of the bank, then resident in Hong Kong in 1920, stated that he wanted a building that would 'dominate the Bund'. [4] Three years later, it was complete. The lions, replicas of which have now been returned to the front of the bank, were commissioned by British sculptors, and became trade marks for the building. The building has now been lovingly restored to its former splendor and serves once more as one of the great landmarks of the city. The evidence for a past deeply linked to finance and logistics can also be seen at Number 6 the Bund, the Russell and Company Building, now home to the flagship store of the modern day Dolce and Gabbana's branch which opened in 2006. Here appearances are deceptive, because while carefully renovated, it is in fact one of the oldest buildings amongst the waterfront stuctures. Russell and Company was in fact a business founded in Guangdong in 1824, before becoming a leading American commercial house in Shanghai. The building that bares its name till today was home to the Imperial Bank of China (which subsequently became the Commercial Bank of China) in May 1897, although other evidence suggests a date of construction back to 1886 or 1881. Prior to this, in the middle of the 19th century, the site was a diplomatic compound with connections to both the Swedish and Norwegian consulates, before being built on for offices for the China Merchants Steam Navigation Company in the 1880s. Between the 1920s and the 1930s it was occupied by Peninsula and Oriental (P and O) Banking. There is another bank at Number 16, the smaller Bank of Taiwan. This structure was completed in 1927 after two years work and housed the Sino-Chinese Bank of Taiwan till 1945. The finance tradition lives on because it became home to the China Merchants Bank in the city in 2006. Another bank stood at Number 18, the Chartered Bank of India, Australia and China, now a slightly smaller building than the two either side of it, but steel framed and in neo-Greek style, designed by a London firm and opened in 1923. At Number 23, the Bank of China rises up, located on the site of a number of previous less ambitious buildings, and finally constructed with 17 floors in 1942. A further building from the stable of Palmer and

---

4. Ibid., p.136.

Turner, made of granite, its vaults were unceremoniously cleared off their gold reserves in May 1949 before the Nationalists left the city. It remains in use as a Bank of China building to this day. At Number 24 is the Yokohama Specie Bank, opened in 1924, and at Number 26 the Yangtsze Insurance Association Building, opened in 1918.

The insurance companies mentioned above signify the major logistics hub that existed in Shanghai from the Qing Dynasty, and which was serviced by these companies. The most powerful symbol on the Bund of its major function as a transport and trade in goods centre is at number 13, the Customs House, with its clock tower that rings out on specific hours over the city to this day. The original building was opened in 1894, as part of the Customs Service established by Sir Robert Hart in the middle of the 19th century, but a new one was constructed in 1924, taking 30 months to complete. It was designed by the famous Palmer and Turner partnership, responsible for many other buildings from this period.

The Bund is also representative of a community that existed at the end of the 19th century and during the first half of the 20th century. Buildings were places to work and do business and statements of economic purpose and pride, but they were also homes or gathering places to Chinese and those outside the country that visited or made the city their home. One of the most popular of these stood at Number Two. The Shanghai Club opened there in 1910, with its iconic six Ionic columns at the centre of the façade. The building was famous in the early part of the last century for its 34 metre black and white marble bar, the renowned 'Long Bar.' The Shanghai Club itself was opened in January 1911. As historian Peter Hibbard explains, 'The Club was Shanghai's unofficial business exchange, and its oak paneled, Jacobean style bar was at it busiest at lunchtimes when customary deals were thrashed out.' [5] Both the noted British actor and playwright Noel Coward, and the famous poet W. H. Auden

---

5. Ibid., p.94.

visited. Derelict for a number of years, it opened as the Waldorf Astoria in 2011, much of its interior lovingly and meticulously restored by the Japanese designer Shimoda Kikutaro. Noel Coward is also linked to the Palace Hotel, next to the great commercial Nanjing Street. Built on the site of what had once been the Central Hotel in 1908. It was here that Sun Yatsen stayed in 1911 after the fall of the Qing Dynasty during the Xinhai Revolution and the establishment of the Republican government. Functioning after 1949 as municipal offices and then a wing of the Peace Hotel, it was transformed in 2010 into the Swatch Arts Peace Hotel. Coward, wrote one of this most celebrated plays, *Private Lives*, in this hotel in the 1930s. The other major social centre was at the Peace Hotel, then known as the northen building of the Palace Hotel, and built as Sassoon House from 1926 to 1929 after one of the great Jewish families came to live in the city. Another of the Palmer and Turner designed buildings, it has a pyramid structure atop making it highly distinctive, and is constructed in an 'A' shape. In the 1930s and 1940s the middle floors of the building housed the famous Cathay Hotel, topped off by a Chinese style ball room and restaurant. From 1949, the building was then the home of the new municipal government, before becoming the Peace Hotel in 1956. Closed in 2007 for three years renovation, it was reopened as a luxury hotel, the Fairmount Peace Hotel. The features which the building had had when it was first opened were fully restored, including some glorious golden murals on the wall, and one of the wooden floored ballrooms.

The Bund was also a centre for media and information in its early phase. Number 17 is occupied by the North China Daily News Building, opened up in 1924 to accommodate the then fifty year old *North China Daily*. Newspapers were particularly important to the first international settlers in the city. 'For most British in the city,' as Hibbard states, 'life without the Far East's leading British newspaper and bastion of the Empire would have been unthinkable.'[6]

---

6. Ibid., p.176.

A predecessor of the American International Group Inc (AIG), the insurance company, occupied part of the building from the 1920s, and, after a lengthy pause, they were to make a comeback there in 1998, occupying the ground floor.

M on the Bund

Going north along Fuzhou Road leading up from the First Zhongshan Road East (the technical name for the street occupied by the Bund buildings) you come on the right to a doorway up some steps. Most nights it is busy here, with people taking the lift up to the fifth or seventh floor, the locations for the M on the Bund restaurant and the Glamour Bar. Both are owned by Australia Michelle Garnaut.

Michelle Garnaut's interest in Shanghai came from a visit she had made to the city first in 1985, when she stayed at the Shanghai Conservatory of Music. Revisiting a decade later in 1995, after she had already established a successful restaurant in Hong Kong, she was persuaded by her restaurant manager to think about having a branch in the city. Originally running one of the restaurants in the old Peace Hotel, she looked at a large number of properties throughout the centre of the city in 1998 before finally taking the plunge and deciding that a location along the Bund was possible. One of the great assets of the NKK building was the expansive view over the rest of the Bund below, and directly to Pudong opposite.

M on the Bund's décor and its cuisine, were to be innovations in Shanghai. But as Garnaut herself pointed out, from the day on which the restaurant opened its newness did not intimidate locals. Chinese clientele often outnumbered those from outside China. She puts this down to the restaurant offering good quality, fairly priced food, good wine, a unique location and good service. But it is also very much built around the personality and food interests of Michelle Garnaut herself, who, despite opening a second branch in Beijing (she closed her Hong Kong branch a few years ago), is often in the restaurant, running a literary festival there and supporting a number of community events. She has also been involved in philanthropy in recent years, funding a village project. Dividing her time between Beijing, Shanghai and Hong Kong, she is able to maintain close interest and management in the venture, and to ensure that the founding values are maintained.

For her, two of the main achievements of the restaurant is that it has been able to bridge the gap which is often perceived between international and local taste, and that it is also able to source excellent ingredients near to the city. For her, this shows that Shanghainese have confidence, are open minded and discerning.

The Future in the Past

The Bund buildings were the homes of companies that were to have a profound effect on the direction of Shanghai's economy in the first half of the 20th century. But some, such as HSBC, which will be described in more detail later, remain active in the city to this day. While others were to disappear, swept away either by political or social or economic change, they built a basis which has not vanished but which provides a foundation on which Shanghai's vision of its future as a trade and finance centre can continue to be built.

One of the most fascinating stories from the earlier period of Shanghai's development which continues to have resonance to this day is that of the Sassoon family, associated with number 20, the Palace Hotel mentioned above. The Sassoons remain one of the world's great dynastic families, and their association with Shanghai occurred at a critical time for them. Their story typifies the ways in which the city supplied, and continues to give entrepreneurs the space to develop their ideas and to engage with the vast market within China. Originating from Iraq before the 18th century, they became active in both India and, a little later, Shanghai. The patriarch, David (1792-1830) was a notable philanthropist and business man with interests that stretched from the Europe to Asia. One of his sons, Elias David (1820-1880) moved to Shanghai from Hong Kong in 1850, and ran a number of businesses there. The most committed to Shanghai however was Victor Sassoon (1881-1961), the founder of the Cathay Hotel, and a tireless supporter of the cause of Jewish refugees coming to the city as a result of the war in Europe. According to one report, 'Victor Sassoon and his countless Shanghai properties – the numbers waver between three and four digits depending on who you ask – spread art deco, modernism and luxury to the city's new age of modernism.'[7] Sassoon left his mark on more than just the Bund in this way. He built the Cathay Complex in the Jin Jiang Hotel, which still serves as the State Guesthouse for the city, the Metropole and Hamilton House on Fuzhou Lu, the Embankment Building on Suzhou Bei Lu, the Cathay Cinema, which remains a theatre to this day, and the Cypress Hotel. 'The key thing about Sassoon was that he changed Shanghai into a modern city overnight, with manners to match.' Peter Hibbard has stated. Sassoon was forced to leave the city during the Japanese occupation, and died in the Bahamas. But his family was perhaps amongst the most legendary from outside China who made the city their home

---

7. Stephanie Thomas, 'Tracking Sassoon's Shanghai Legacy', CNN, 30 November 2010

and did business there, and architecturally they had a lasting impact. More than this, however, they also created the sense that Shanghai was a global and international city, not just a domestic centre and logistics hub. That legacy lives on.

The companies that were housed in the Bund buildings were also critical to the fortunes of the city during this early period of global economic development. Some like NKK and the Standard Bank were to build the first finance sector in the city, and were part of the infrastructure that also supported a stock exchange. The existence of a port and a shipping sector meant that insurance and other services connected to the global economy as it existed then developed. It was for this reason that so many foreign business people came to the city to make their fortune, many of them working, playing and living along the Bund.

Today there is also something else that the Bund collection of great buildings testifies to. Almost all of them in the last two decades have been transformed, renovated, modernized. They are not dead remnants of a former period, a sort of museum, but living, vital components of the modern society, heritage and identity of the city. Far from being overshadowed by the Pudong skyline above, they attract as much attention at night, when they are lit up, with great groups of tourists from China and overseas walking along the promenade. Their shops are some of the most fashionable in the city, their hotels some of the most exclusive. This is best symbolized by the announcement on the 20th July by the Shanghai Municipality Huangpu District of the proposal to create a Bund Financial Innovation Centre. This would be part of the implementation of a national programme to support financial services development in Shanghai. It would provide support for the development of a services sector in the area, and tighter regulatory supervision, particularly for private companies in finance. Shanghai's aspirations to create an international finance sector will be looked at in Chapter Six. And its experience of regeneration in Chapter Seven. Innovation and creativity in both these areas will be important in order to achieve the

City's objectives of building a modern multi-centred urban area by 2020. The Bund, therefore, continue to function in the 21st century as a place of innovation and development as they did in the previous hundred and fifty years. They are both historic monuments but also testify to the present and the future.

Chapter Two

The Opening Up of the City from 1990

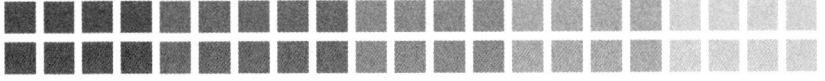

Shanghai has always been a major industrial centre and has played a key part as China has modernized its economy, both before and after 1949. According to one Shanghai based economist, from 1949 to 1978 the city supported half of China's manufacturing and a third of its fiscal revenues, and supplied half of industrial value added growth for the whole country.[1] From the start of the economic reforms in 1978 to 1990, however, the city has existed in a different economic context. During this period, in order to stimulate the economy, the concept of Special Economic Zones was promulgated, with a raft of preferential policies initially extended to them from 1980 onwards. This made them more competitive and productive during the early phase of opening up. The impact of this means that over this period, Shanghai's proportional contribution to the country's economy declined.

This is not a straightforward story. It is no longer about raw statistics. The economy which Shanghai plays a role in now is radically different to that which existed thirty years ago. Those who visit the city now see an economy that is positioning itself to be the most service-sector orientated, middle income driven in the whole of the country. They are seeing somewhere which offers what one analyst called a vision of what 'the future of consumption in China'[2] might look like and which another

---

1. Interview, Shanghai, 5 November 2012
2. Interview, Hong Kong, 1 November 2012

said is 'moving faster to the frontier of China's economy'. The competitive advantages of Shanghai in this new context, as this and the following chapter on the economy will make clear, are human capital, the openness of the city to foreign capital and multinational companies, the exposure that the city's companies have to the outside world, its logistic advantages and the improving environment of the city for living.

Special Economic Zones

One of the key policy innovations from 1978 when the post-Mao Zedong leadership established itself was the idea of allowing more space for non-state business activity, and liberalizing laws which allowed foreign capital to come into China. The first joint venture law was passed in 1979, and the first proper joint venture company was a Coca Cola bottling plant in Tianjin. From 1980, a series of Special Economic Zones were set up, of which Shenzhen, Zhuhai and Xiamen were amongst the first. These leveraged off their position occupying key geographical locations facing Hong Kong, Macau and Taiwan respectively, which offered access to markets, technology and capital through the businesses located there. Throughout the 1980s, Hong Kong enterprises came in increasing numbers to establish factories in Shenzhen in particular, creating goods for the export market. From 1996 Shenzhen was then allowed to create goods for the internal market too.

Special Economic Zones were one of the Deng Xiaoping leadership's key achievements. They were successful not only because they combined good locations with a strong economic rationale for growth, but also because they offered, in a manageable and easily controllable way, a way to experiment with growth-supporting policies. A wholesale opening up of the country with its widely different regional economies and dynamics would have been hugely risky, not least because engagement with foreign enterprises had been so limited and shallow prior to the 1980s. Allowing staged entrepreneurialism meant that the local and national governments were able to implement specific experimental policies, see if they were successful, then take things to the next stage. This 'crossing the river by feeling the stones' became a useful template for many other areas of policy.

Shanghai was not one of the initial group of places designated as Special Economic Zone and did not enter their family till 1991. Its economy prior to this had been heavily dominated by major manufacturing state owned industries. Some of these were in automotive and light machinery. The Shanghai Automotive Company still exists, and was a major employer in the city. It typified the 'work unit' model from this time – an entity which provided not just work but social welfare, accommodation, housing, and a whole world in which its employees and their families lived, often all their lives. There were other large state companies making the bedrock of the economy in the city, from those in shipping, to those in retail and food production.

But there was another history of enterprise in the city, going back to the period before 1949 when small companies, many of them artisans, existed. Some of these had survived but their activities were relatively modest by the 1980s. The explosion of town and village enterprises, semi private vehicles in a variety of sectors, swept the rest of the country, seeing major improvements in the efficiency of agricultural production and the introduction of a new entrepreneurial culture in rural areas in the 1980s, but Shanghai's growth in this period was driven by industrialization and state capital investment.

The decision to finally make Shanghai a special zone in 1990 was triggered by a realization that a new phase of economic liberalism needed to be launched. The fall of the Soviet Union that year only underlined how important strong economic growth policies were for political stability. The moribund Soviet industrial model had in the end collapsed through mismanagement and inefficiency, with stagnant growth levels and rising public dissatisfaction. The need to promote more areas for faster growth within China returned to the leaders' minds, and in 1990, Pudong area, south of the Puxi river, till then dominated by warehouses and small factories, along with farmland, was declared the final Special Economic Zone (SEZ), the 15th since 1980. As an SEZ it was accorded preferential tax policies, foreign capital could be more easily deployed in the city, and joint ventures were able to make goods for export with preferential tariffs.

One of the key motives behind granting this status was to recognize the city's excellent geographical location, and the fact that it stood on the confluence of the Huangpu River as it runs into the South China Sea. It enjoyed a port that was able at lease to accommodate up to medium sized container ships that were then able to ship outwards to the local export markets in South Korea and Japan, and from there to the US and Europe. Beyond this, the port was a place for inward shipment of goods that could be bought in partly finished, then processed and re-exported.

Urban Planning and the Development of the City

Before 1990, however, there had been a number of former strategies and processes by which the city was built and developed. Urban planning has been a feature of the city's development for several decades, and it is within the framework of these plans and the priorities that they have spelled out that modern Shanghai has developed. Already the home to most of the country's industrial assets in the 1920s, Sun Yat-Sen was to state in 1922 in 'Nation Building Strategies: Industrial Planning' that 'if Shanghai keeps developing like this, it will not be able to meet the requirements of a world commercial port.'[3] The Shanghai Municipal Government was formally established in July 1927 to better manage the port and the surrounding area. Three years later, 'Contents for Planning a Big Shanghai' was issued by the Shanghai Downtown Construction Committee, looking at developing the traffic systems, logistics and infrastructure of the metropolitan area. As a result of this plan, a number of roads were built. After the end of the Sino Japanese War in 1945 the City's Construction and Engineering Bureau formulated plans for the reconstruction of the city after its devastation by the previous decade of war and conflict. In August 1946, an Urban Planning Committee was formally established, issuing a Great Shanghai Urban Plan in February 1948, which was approved in 1949 on the establishment of the People's Republic of China, and then formally published in 1950. Part of this plan was the zoning of the city into residential, commercial and political areas, something that was to typify cities across the newly established Republic. The focal points for Shanghai were for it to become a harbor and commercial city and to leverage on its position before 1940 as a major international commercial and logistics centre. These early plans attempted to create green areas for recreation, an urban railway system, and an airport.

In 1953, a USSR expert was pointed to draw up a master plan for the further development of the city. This attempted to introduce modern concepts of urban planning, mixing residential, commercial

---

3. Wujun Liu; Xiang Huang. *Shanghai Urban Planning*. Shanghai Century Publishing Co. Ltd., 2007

and recreational zones. It was also tried to deal with a rising urban population, and to develop the port and harbor areas. It managed industrial areas, by bunching industrial use buildings into concentrated areas. A decision by the State Council in Beijing in 1958 approved transfer of ten counties to the Shanghai area from neighbouring Jiangsu province. These included Baoshan, Jiading and Songjiang.[4] As a result of work between the Shanghai Municipal Committee and the Urban Planning Committee within the Ministry of Construction and Engineering, 'Preliminary Suggestions on the Master City Plan of Shanghai,' which suggested placing controls on the development of suburban areas and reconstructing the old downtown area was put forward.

The first Master Plan to be approved by the Central Government, however, did not appear until 1986. The 1986 master plan proposed the following core areas for development:

1. Developing the Pudong area

2. Developing satellite towns

3. Constructing and rebuilding the central area

4. Developing the south bank of the estuary of the Yangtze River and the north bank of Hangzhou bay

5. Constructing small towns in the suburbs.

One of the major results of this 1986 plan was the creation of a formal 'Master Plan for the Development of the Pudong New Area.'

---

4. Ibid.

The Opening Up of the City from 1990

Pudong

Pudong is meaningful in capturing the aspirations and desire for futurism and change for the city because it physically embodies and illustrates this. Change here is not abstract, but actually happens before your eyes. Sitting in one of the coffee shops or restaurants across from the Pudong water front on the Bund as the light fades and evening comes on, one of the most dramatic sight in the modern world is the way in which slowly the whole of the city-scape comes to life, with lights and illuminations stretching across the modern buildings before you, some of them carrying adverts, others slogans, and others vast and colourful images which stretch sometimes from one building to the other, marching across the sky. Sometimes there are dramatic clouds that rise above all this, tinged with artificial light; sometimes the Huangpu river is so alive with ships going up and down the water, with their noise and bustle, that it offers a slight distraction to the drama of light before you. Whatever weather this view is seen in, it is always impressive to see who are visitors to the city for the first time. They go quiet as they absorb what they are seeing, trying to take in all the change and energy and dynamism, their eyes working across the buildings before them. It is even more striking to then tell them that all of this was only built up from the early 1990s. Before that, they would be standing here looking out over low buildings, without light, warehouses and farming structures. That was all that was here before 1990.

The development of Pudong from that year was symbolic of the city's aspirations to its future economic status and of its opening up. As the raft of former Master Plans and other documents outlined above makes clear, however, this was an event with lengthy antecedents. Six years earlier, in 1984, the Shanghai Municipal Government had already proposed that Pudong area be developed. This was put to the national State Council in 1985. The then Mayor of Shanghai, Jiang Zemin, stated in support of this bid that:

'Shanghai as a well known metropolis had by the 1930s developed into one of the most important trading and financial centres in Asia. Since 1949, much emphasis has been put on economic development. However, due to various reasons the development and renewal of our city have lagged behind, thereby weakening the function of Shanghai as an economic centre and as a hub for other parts of the country. This situation obviously cannot be allowed to continue. Various means were adopted in the past to renew old city area, but results have not been cost-effective. A new direction, therefore, has been taken which comprises two parts; namely, the renewal of old districts and the simultaneous development of new districts. As the biggest city in the country and occupying the most important position, it is totally in line with party policy to further reform, open up and develop Pudong, and to expedite the development of Shanghai's economy into one that is externally orientated and to build a new district that is international and that performs the function of a nerve centre. This plan, therefore, must be properly implemented.' [5]

In 1988, in order to facilitate this vision, a leading group for the development of the Pudong area was formed. Two years later in April 1990, this body endorsed a report from the Shanghai Government for the development of the area, resulting in a comprehensive Pudong Development Plan, and a new Pudong Development Leading Group, alongside a Development Office. Ten years after the establishment of the first Special Economic Zones, on 30 April 1990 the area was formally named as a special development area. Preferential policies were allowed in the following areas:

1. Income tax for foreign investors

---

5. "Develop Shanghai's Pudong New Area", *Selected Works of Jiang Zemin*, Eng. ed., FLP, Beijing, 2010, Vol.I, p.34−35.

2. Customs duties and tax for equipment, vehicles and building materials from foreign investment

3. Making foreign investment support export orientated industry

4. Allowing foreign investment in infrastructure projects in the area

5. Allowing foreign investors to operate tertiary industries

6. Allowing foreign banks to open branches in the area

7. Opening up a foreign free trade zone

8. Preferential treatment for income tax reduction to be given to enterprises conforming to industrial policies which add value to Pudong's development

9. Allowing leases for land of 50 to 70 years, and allowing foreigners to partake in this

10. Allowing Pudong to keep revenues for the area for further development

Flowing from this, 9 regulations and guidelines were set up to support the preferential policies, which flowed through three development companies:

The Waigaoqiao Free Trade Zone

The Lujiazui Financial and Trade Zone

The Jinqiao Export Processing Zone

Blue prints were offered for how Pudong might be physically developed, with the British architect Richard Rogers presenting a hub and spoke plan for a city dependent on public transport. In fact, the city had to make a less structured plan, largely through the need to sign up specific developers to build particular projects. Within a decade, the city had skyscrapers, the Oriental Television tower which was the tallest structure in China for most of the 1990s after it was completed in 1994, and new hotels, office blocks and streets.

The creation of a special economic zone in the city had an immense energizing impact on growth. This is clear in a whole number of statistics plotting the changes over the ensuing two decades. In 1990, the population of Shanghai was 13 million. By 2011, it had nearly doubled to 23 million, an addition of a quarter of a million people a year. Gross domestic product in 1990 was RMB 78 billion. By 2011 it had sky rocketted to RMB 1.9 trillion. Per capita GDP in 1990 was RMB 5911. By 2011 it had risen to RMB 82 thousand. The number of contracts for Foreign Direct Investment in 1990 was 203. By 2011, it had risen to 4329. Contractual foreign investment in 1990 was USD 200 million. By 2011, this had gone to USD 20 billion, a hundred fold increase. In 1990, the city transported through its ports and its airport at that time 228 million tons of goods. In 2011, this was 933 million. Passenger departures had risen from 38 million to 135 million. In 1990, there were 450 thousand households with telephones installed. By 2011, this had risen to 9 million. 890 thousand foreign visitors came to the city in 1990. Within two decades, this had risen tenfold to 8 million. The city's population grew 76 per cent from 1990 to 2011, and its GDP 9 times what it had been before. Foreign direct investment had grown 20 times over this period, and per capita annual disposable income for urban households 17 times. The total value of imports and exports into the city had shot up 57 times, with imports increasing 100 fold, and exports 38 times. The most rapid growth was seen in the decade 1990 to 2000, when the city was rising from a relatively low base level, but the momentum of this change was maintained over the following decade.[6]

This is most clearly visible in the growth of GDP. Below is a table to GDP growth rates for the city over the last two decades. The strongest rises were in the period 1992 to 2007. The table also has total investment in fixed assets, which shows that over the opening

---

6. Zhixiong Wang; Junxian Ma. *Shanghai Statistical Yearbook 2012*. China Statistics Press, Beijing, 2012, pp.4–7.

phase of the development of Pudong the city saw major capital investment into infrastructure, with 1993 posting a staggering rise of 83 per cent.

Table: Growth Rate for GDP and Total Investment in Fixed Assets 1990-2011

Year	Gross Domestic Product	Total Investment in Fixed Assets
1990	3.5	5.7
1991	7.1	13.7
1992	14.8	38.4
1993	15.1	83.0
1994	14.5	71.8
1995	14.3	42.6
1996	13.1	21.9
1997	12.8	1.3
1998	10.3	-0.6
1999	10.4	-5.5
2000	11.0	0.7
2001	10.5	6.7
2002	11.3	9.6
2003	12.3	12.1
2004	14.2	25.8
2005	11.4	14.8
2006	12.7	10.8
2007	15.2	13.6
2008	9.7	8.3
2009	8.2	9.2
2010	10.3	0.8
2011	8.2	0.3

From *Shanghai Statistical Yearbook 2012*. p.15

Shanghai 2020

■■■■■■■■■■■■■■■■■■■■

A Walk through Pudong in the 21st Century

Shanghai Pudong now contains some of the world's most impressive modern skyscrapers. As with the buildings along the Bund which faces them across the river, each one of these tells a story about the development of the area and the ways in which the city is articulating its economic future through innovation and investment in the built environment in the 21st century.

Shanghai World Financial Centre was designed by American firm Kohn Pederson Fox and developed by the Japanese Mori Building Company. It houses hotels, offices, conference rooms, and shopping malls. The main hotel is the Park Hyatt, from the 79th to the 93rd floors, currently the world's second highest hotel. Completed in September 2007 after a decade of building, at 492 metres it was at the time the tallest building in China and the second tallest in the world. The signature of the building is the oblong placed in the very top of the structure. The total floor count is 101 stories.

The Jin Mao Building next door, comes in at 88 stories, and consists of offices and the Grand Hyatt Hotel (which, in the early 2000s, had been the highest hotel in the world). Designed by Chicago based architects Skidmore, Owings and Merrill, it is divided into 16 segments giving it a pagoda-like look. Opened in 1998, it was, for almost nine years, the tallest building in China, and the fifth tallest in the world. Inside, the most distinctive feature is the atrium for the hotel, which looks up over thirty floors to swirling shapes reaching to the top floors.

The Bank of Shanghai Headquarters with 46 floors was completed in 2005, by the architects Kenzo Tange Associates.

The Bank of China Tower with its oval encased dark central tower rising from two shorter lighter coloured flanking towers is 53 stories tall, and was completed in 2000, again by a Japanese architect practice, Nikken Sekkei.

The Bocom Financial Towers are neighbouring towers of different heights connected by an atrium. The north tower is 230 metres tall and the south 197 tall. They were designed by the ABB Architekten. The north tower was completed in 2002 after four years of work, and the south tower in 1999 after two years.

The International Ocean Shipping Building took two years to build from 1998 to 2000, with 50 floors. It is multi functional, with offices, hotels, restaurants, and retail. It was designed by the East China Architectural Design and Research Institute and Joseph Bogdan Associates Ltd.

While each of these buildings are radically different in design, function and size to those from the start of the 20th century on the north side of the Huangpu River, they have one common aspect – they were built by an international collection of architects, and in many cases pioneered new techniques or designs.

■■■■■■■■■■■■■■■■■■■■■■

Pudong in the second decade of the 21st century stands for the rewards and the limits of modernity in China. On the one hand, one can walk around the city and feel the immense industriousness and energy of the place. One can see globalization through the presence of foreign enterprises, foreign brands and through the ways in which people walk around dressed as they would be in New York or Paris or Sydney or London, living the same kind of life styles as people there. One can see the heavy presence of Chinese and foreign financial enterprises and an idea of the ways in which the city is at the forefront of China's strategy to become a more diverse, service orientated economy. But there are also other less positive things; the dominance by this area of the city of the car, and the need to create a more pedestrian friendly landscape; the need for more green open spaces, and for a city that is more sustainable. Some of the skyscrapers have been built to new standards of greenness and sustainability. Seeing this experimentation is encouraging. The diversity of architectural styles hints at a deeper and more authentic Chinese vision of modernity. A city in the future with a stronger visual sign of community, with less reliance on cars and with more diversity would be a good aspiration. In the next decade too, it is important to move beyond the rhetoric of hoping to create a cultural centre to realizing this with more diverse cultural entities and the lives and economies they support. In short, a stronger sense that Pudong is not just an economic community, but a human one.

The Shanghai Stock Exchange

In one area, Shanghai has played a critical part in the development of the modern Chinese economy: the financial services sector. Financial services barely existed as a concept from 1949 onwards, with banks and finance sector companies operated on a monopoly basis by the state. Shanghai boasts one of China's two stock markets, and perhaps the earliest. Established in December 1990, it was authorized before that of the Stock Exchange in Shenzhen, but did not start activity till after Shenzhen's. Shanghai stock exchange had its roots in a meeting held by the then Major of Shanghai, Jiang Zemin, in August 1986 when he convened a meeting to discuss industrial reform. One of the challenges was how to find more inventive ways of raising capital and introducing efficiency into the state owned enterprises that still employed so many but which were so dependent on state finance that this was seen as stifling their economic energy. Modest shareholding experiments, largely to employees of particular enterprises, were formally sanctioned, and in September 'Over the Counter shares' (OTC) started trading at the Shanghai Jing'an branch of the Industrial and Commercial Bank of China in West Nanjing Road. As Stephen Green, in his history of the Chinese stock market states, 'Along with a similar OTC in Shenyang in Liaoning Province, China's current stock market was born.' [7] This enjoyed very modest growth in the ensuing few years, with only nine companies listed by mid-1989. But while Party Secretary and Mayor of Shanghai in the late 1980s and early 1990s, Zhu Rongji has seen the use of a stock exchange in the ideas of how to redevelop Pudong. Receiving both Chen Yun and Deng Xiaoping's support, the formal stock exchange began operation in December 1990. [8]

The early phase of the development of the stock exchange in the 1990s was difficult. Few companies issued shares, and the legal infrastructure did not exist to accelerate or promote the radical expansion of a market. In November 1991, then Premier Li Peng visited the Shanghai Stock Exchange and wrote 'The stock exchange serves socialist economic construction.' But the question of just how easy it would be to combine socialism with an entity that symbolised capitalism would prove not so easy to settle. Even during Deng Xiaoping's Southern Tour in early 1992, he was to state: 'What about our stock market? Is it socialist or capitalist? To decide, we must experiment first. If the experiment is a success, it can be popularized. If problems arise, we can close it.' [9]

The Shanghai and Shenzhen stock market never closed, so we can assume the experiment has been a success. Within a decade, they had over 1200 firms listed, with capitalization of USD 150 billion. 'The market had become an important source of financing for State Owned Enterprises (SOEs) and an important contributor to

---

7. Stephen Green. *China's Stockmarket: A Guide to Its Progress, Players and Prospects*. The Economist/Profile Books, London, 2003. p.1.
8. Ibid., p.12.
9. Ibid., p.13.

the state's fiscal revenues.'[10] Part of this development was because the political issued about the place of a stock market in a socialist economic system alluded to above had been addressed. In 1993, at the 14th Party Congress, the idea was accepted as part of the process of state owned enterprise reform that SOEs should be restructured and modernized, with more of a separation between state and management functions. As part of this reform, they were compelled to raise capital either from banks or from other sources rather than being wholly reliant on state funds. In 1997, the central government recognized that the stock market was 'an important component of the national economy' with the then President and Party Secretary Jiang Zemin stating that it has become 'an essential part of the socialist market economy.' Partly, this was also because the ways in which the stock exchange was able to deliver efficiencies in the allocation of capital and the means by which large state owned enterprises were managed and directed had become clear to Zhu Rongji and others as the 1990s wore on. A proper regulatory authority was set up and greater definition given to the types of shares that could be owned, and the ways in which they could be traded. How the stock exchange has developed since entry to the World Trade Organisation in 2001 will be looked at in the chapter on Shanghai as a finance centre.

Planning the Future: The 2001 Master Plan

From 1992, after the Central Government made the decision to support Shanghai as it became a global city, there was renewed urgency to create a place with a radically different function to that

---

10. Ibid.

which had existed before. In May 2000, the State Council approved a Master City Plan for Shanghai to run from 1999 to 2020. This document built on the success of Pudong's redevelopment since 1990, and aimed to focus on building Shanghai into an economic, financial and trading centre within the next two decades. The slogan was to 'rejuvenate Shanghai, develop Pudong, serve China and open up to the world.'

• Serving China and Opening Up to the World: Historically, Shanghai's geographical position meant it had always been a portal between the vast inland areas of China and the rest of Asia and the world. The 1999-2020 plan explicitly recognized this by supporting the concept that Shanghai had a prominent role not just in the regional but in the global economy and needed to look at itself as both a Chinese or Asian city, but also as a global city.

• Development of the Urban and Suburban Areas: Shanghai's urban area of over 6000 square kilometers meant it needed to look beyond its historic centre by the Puxi and develop multi-nodal settings. Suburbs had to be created with all the community and business functions to be self sustaining but also integrated with each other.

• Unified and Co-ordinated Development: The city authorities had to accept some of the principles of a free market, and of organic and localized growth across the city – but they also had to balance these against the energy, food and sustainability agendas of the city as a whole. In this sense, Shanghai operates as a microcosm of China as a whole – trying to find a happy medium between centralization in some administrative functions, but listening to local ideas on others.

• Taking People as the Key: This had been a phrase originally from ancient Qin philosophy over two and a half millennium before – the idea that the prime role of government is to take people at the heart of all its considerations and strategies, and defining carefully how best to serve them. The city in this objective set out part of its sustainability and developmental objectives – to become a diverse, multi faceted mixed economy and community in the next two decades.

- Preserving Tradition while Innovating: As this book has already described, Shanghai had an historic heritage, along the Puxi and in many of the concessions into which the city had been split as it had developed as a port in the 19th and early 20th century. For this objective of both preserving and innovating, the city set out its strategic objective of recognizing the importance of looking after this heritage while also ensuring it was used in a modern context and did not stagnate.

The 1999-2020 plan wrestles with many problems generic across the whole of China. One of these is the efficient and sustainable use of land. In its development, Shanghai had lost much rural land for building factories, houses and offices. 97 per cent of its food is now brought in from other cities (see the chapter on sustainability and the economy). Water use had become critical because of the sharp rises in people living in the urban area. Pollution had risen because of rising car use, despite the fact that some factories had now moved away from the city. There were issues of social cohesion because of the dramatic influx of new people from various areas both in the country and in the whole region. The development plan therefore had to be underpinned by issues of sustainability in terms of land use, resources use and management of large inflows of new residents. With these objectives in mind, the 1999-2020 plan set the following objectives:

- Internationalising the city
- Integrating urban and rural areas and their respective economies in the municipal area
- Supporting environmental sustainability
- Building modern infrastructure
- Supporting social cohesion

In terms of the implementation, the plan set out the following specific steps:

- Expansion of Shanghai's coastal development, with the building of waterfront cities like Baoshan and Waigaoqiao, and the development of Chongming Island

- Developing a multi-axel city, running through Shanghai-Ningbo, Shanghai-Hangzhou, and the riverside axes

- Developing the layout of the central city, with a reorganization of the parks, residential areas and commercial spaces. This will be looked at later

- The creation of a Central Business District in Liujiazui running into Pudong, on the model of other international cities

- Creation of open spaces, for recreation, such as the People's Square

- Planning industrial development so that it develops higher valued industries and its service sector (see section on Five Year Plan below)

- Development of intercity connections through the construction of fast train routes so that the city is linked to important local cities close to it like Hangzhou, Ningbo and Nanjing

- Development of information technology to assist local industry

- Development of the road infrastructure

- Control and protection of the environment and water resources in the city, and prevention of air pollution

- Efficient waste management

- Protection of historic spaces

- Development of the human capital through investment in education, both at primary and tertiary level, and the support of Shanghai's universities in becoming world class research and teaching institutes

- Development of Shanghai as a cultural centre, with attention paid to the soft and hard infrastructure of culture through both building theatres, concert halls, libraries and other cultural centres and also encouraging the city to become an international centre for performances and creativity

- Improvements of the local health care system, so that some of the imbalances that have existed since reform and opening up started between world class facilities for some and poor or non existent health care for others is corrected

- Building up the social welfare and social security system to deal with the impact of uneven development and rapid change in society which had been one of the outcomes of the economic growth in the last decades

- Improving the infrastructure to supply water, gas, and electricity, and moving to sustainable or renewable forms of energy

- Ensuring the city has an adequate crisis management system in place

The 1999-2020 Plan set out the key strategic objectives for the city in the first two decades of the 20th century. Within this period, the central government had stated that it wished to see China become a middle income country, with per capita GDPs of over USD 10,000 in this period. The term 'harmonious development' used in the first few years of the new century underlined how important the issues of balance and stability were as China nationally progressed towards becoming a more wealthy, more developed society. But there were plenty of challenges as it went along this path. Shanghai in many ways, as the City Plan made clear, had to face these issues within its own municipal area.

One of the key concepts in this plan is that with a city covering over 600 square kilometers and nearly 25 million people, there was a

The Opening Up of the City from 1990

need to create a multi centred city, with less emphasis on the concept of one down town area, and a process of decentralization. This was aimed at taking the strain off transport networks, and building up a form of social cohesion. At least people in smaller and more localized communities have a stronger sense of belonging somewhere and their responsibilities as members of these areas. The city has also supported a process of reusing formerly industrial land for residential or open space use. There is a critical need in these suburbs for open spaces and for more green. In that sense, Shanghai's model is to become more like Sydney or London in being almost a city of villages. One of the most interesting new developments has been the Songjiang New Town, developed as part of the 'One city, nine towns' strategy, and covering 60 square kilometers housing half a million people. This has a number of new residential communities including the Thames Town area, with housings and community buildings constructed in what is considered a classically English style. It also has a film studio, a university and a new hospital. These new areas are a pragmatic move, but are major experiments, and they will only show their success if they are able to develop as communities with their own momentum and dynamism rather than being products of state mandated planning.

Shanghai and the Five Year Plans

The 1999-2020 Plan shows how important it is to see Shanghai's development within a national, and not just a local, context. This is underlined when on looks at the ways in which Shanghai's development in the last two decades has linked to the Five Year Programmes. China has issued Five Year Programmes (although they were called Plans till the 2000s) since it adopted the state run economic model from the Soviet Union in 1953. Its key objective in the early years was to create a transition from agricultural to industrial production.[11] What is often forgotten is that from 1953 to 1978, under the initial plans, Chinese GDP growth rose an average of 5 to 6 per cent per year.

1978 marks a watershed not just in the economic configuration of China, with an acceptance of the market (with Chinese characteristics – what the senior leader Chen Yun called, in the 1980s, the 'bird in the cage' model) and of non state enterprises, but also in a change in the emphasis on the Plans. What originally functioned as key elements in the Command economy, prescribing down to small details the delivery objectives of the Chinese macro-economy became, from this 1978, what we would understand in the West as broader statements of political-economic intent, setting out parameters by which the national and provincial governments of the PRC can conduct their short to medium term economic policy, while allowing increasing space for enterprise.

In the period of the 10th Five Year Programme from 2001 to 2005 the key objectives for the city were:

- Initially form the economic scale and comprehensive strength of a world metropolis
- Optimise urban spatial distribution
- Begin the first stages of modernising the city's physical infrastructure
- Participate more deeply in the international economy
- Pursue balanced social, economic and environmental development

---

11. *History of the Communist Party of China: 1949 to 1978*, Central Committee Historical Research Publishing House, Beijing, 2011, Volume I, pp.6-11.

In terms of industrial development over this period, the Tenth Five Year Programme' proposed:

- Developing major industries to boost growth
- Nurturing new and high tech industries to become engines of future growth
- Transform the traditional industries and develop petrochemicals, iron and steel
- Encourage greater employment and metropolitan style industries
- Improve industrial relocation and readjust spatial economic distribution

We find in the 11th Five Year Programme from 2006 to 2010, therefore, many of the themes of the 12th one – a commitment to growth rates above 8 per cent (in fact, despite the global economic crisis from 2008 onwards, China overall managed to post over 10 per cent growth over this period, outdelivering on its stated promise in 2006) and to improving energy efficiency, research and development levels, spending on welfare, addressing inequality and creating an innovation and enterprise culture.

The 12th Five Year Programme was adopted at a time of great change in the global economy. The ramifications of the global financial crisis are still with us. China has emerged in a more powerful and influential position than it had before. China's contributions to global growth, through the large stimulus package of 2008-09, were significant in maintaining overall global growth and preventing a much more serious global depression. But the financial crisis still shook the global economy to the core. In 2013, Europe continues to face a major problem over debt in the Euro zone, and again China has indicated that it is prepared to help where necessary and where it can. But the effects of the global crisis were also significant for China, with the sudden drop off in import demand from the developed world especially in 2008 into 2009. Rising international prices for energy and raw materials generally also contributed to new increasing levels of inflation. The 12th five year programme nationally and at the municipal level in Shanghai was formulated therefore against the background of an increasingly uncertain international environment.

The key themes of the 12th Five Year Programme are:

- Promoting industrial upgrading by scientific innovation
- Strengthening the technical improvement of enterprises
- Building reliable and recognisable brands
- Helping in the creation of a healthy competitive environment where multi-national companies (MNCs) work with, alongside and in partnership with small and medium enterprises
- Optimising the development of business services – how the diversification of retail outlets can support communities and community developments
- Delivering in partnership between MNCs and local and national government energy efficiency and on the creation of a sustainable, green economy
- Developing and opening up the Shanghai Pudong New Area, in creating an international finance centre, but one suitable for China's national conditions, and one where there can be a harmonious balance between the imperatives of Western MNCs and Chinese partners and stakeholders (this will be dealt with in detail in the chapter on the International Finance Centre)

The key highlights of the 12th Five Year programme, therefore, are not so much the commitment to growth. The World Bank, the International Monetary Fund (IMF), and most other observers, see the likelihood of positive growth in the Chinese economy over the next five years as very high. The slightly lowered objective of seeing Gross Domestic Product (GDP) increase year on year by 7 per cent is, barring catastrophe, pretty certain. What is more important is the stress in the Programme on nurturing sustainable growth, ensuring the quality of growth (and we read that as meaning looking to rebalance from export led to domestic sources of growth, and going up the value train in terms of manufacturing), a commitment to creating strong financial services infrastructure (and in this area, Shanghai is a key player), and creating more space for innovation, research and development and training. The 12th Five Year Programme, therefore, is the strongest yet in supporting a knowledge economy, and in driving China towards its stated goal of being a middle income country by 2020, with a per capita GDP of around USD 7 to 8000. It needs to be stressed that with one of the highest per capita GDPs in China, therefore, Shanghai municipality (with a rate of USD 9 to 12 thousand per capita) fulfils the function within this national plan of being an important incubator, particularly in the areas of knowledge-driven economic growth, the expansion of the green economy, and the creation of an international financial centre acting as an interface between China and the rest of the world.

The programme also marks an important shift in the overall direction of economic policy for China. One of the key themes it addresses is the need to develop the service economy as the country gradually moves away from the previous model of growth which was heavily dependent on massive government investment and (relatively) cheap manufacturing export (according to US economist Barry Naughton, in the last two decades, over 44 per cent of GDP has been in fixed capital investment, a remarkably high figure, even in a developing economy).[12] China is now seeking to move further up the value chain as its economy reforms and modernises but also crucially to rely to a greater extent on domestic consumption as one of the key drivers for future, and long term sustainable, economic growth. This element of the plan will be particularly applicable to the more modern and developed sectors of the economy along the eastern seaboard which were the engines of China's growth in the past. There will be radical

---

12. Barry Naughton. *The Chinese Economy*. Massachusetts Institute of Technology Press, 2007.

implications for employment and training. New skills will need to be developed. There will also be substantive changes necessary to the behaviour of households who will need both the means and the will to engage in a more consumer led economy. To back all this up, there needs to be, as the programme recognises, a more highly developed welfare system on which people can rely.

Shanghai's Own Programme 2011-2015

Many of these themes are picked up in Shanghai's own Five Year Programme, which in many respects mirrors the national programme, but reflects and builds on Shanghai's special position at the forefront of the modern economy in China. Shanghai envisages an average growth rate of 8 per cent, slightly above the national level in the next five years from 2011, but well in keeping with the advanced nature of its economy. The core of Shanghai's vision in the programme during this period is to further develop the city as one with four key central economic platforms:

- To make Shanghai an economic centre
- To make the city a finance centre
- To make the city a trade centre
- To make the city a transport centre

These are part of an integrated strategic plan. Economic development has to continue, with what the central government calls 'fast, sustainable growth' — that is to say, growth that continues to deliver

The Opening Up of the City from 1990

jobs and satisfy the aspirations of people living in the city. Shanghai has to develop a mixed economy to achieve this, but also create an innovative, dynamic model that raises the levels of the service sector in the economy and delivers rising consumption so that the city can become a source of growth within itself. To become a finance sector will be a subject dealt with at some length later. It is clear that Shanghai is positioning itself at the forefront of the financial services sector in China, and the interface between the vast potential domestic market and the outside world. This is why banks, insurance companies and providers of financial services in the city, domestically and internationally, are increasing. Shanghai through all this however will not change from its current and historic position as a trade centre, a place where people come to do diverse forms of business, and somewhere where companies wish to set up offices, employ people, but and sell. Finally, the city has physically an enormous asset in the huge ports, currently the busiest in the world, and in the road and transport infrastructure. Shanghai aims in the next decade to become a hub where people can arrive efficiently and where they can undertake business easily. This means deeper links with the outside world. These are the four fundamental structures on which Shanghai's vision of its future are built.

In November 2012, in a media interview, Zhou Zhenhua, director of the Development Research Center of Shanghai Municipal People's Government, talked about his understanding of Shanghai's 12th Five Year Programme. Creativity and innovation are at the heart of its plans, making use of new technologies, developing the knowledge economy and transforming the economic system so that by the end of the period there is commitment to a figure of over 65% per cent of Shanghai's GDP comes from the service industries. Again mirroring the national programme, Shanghai envisages substantial investment in research and development (R and D), setting a target of spending on R and D of 3.3% of GDP by the end of the period. This will go along with a renewed emphasis on training a better educated work force with the aim of 35 per cent of the workforce having got a Senior Middle School qualification or above. Interaction with the outside world will be a vital component in this process and Shanghai will be positively encouraging foreign enterprises and expertise to locate to the city. Shanghai's prosperity is founded on its position as a major trading port, and its future will equally depend to some real extent on its interaction with the globalising economy. The local programme envisages that a further 100 MNCs will be located there over the next five years and wants to build the higher education sector as very much the go-to place for foreign students wishing to study in China.

The Key Areas of the 12th Five Year Programme

It is worth looking briefly at the detail of what the Five Year Programme offers in specific areas, and in particular look at international practice and what can be learned from this or adopted from it as China and Shanghai embark on the next phase of their development. These will be covered in more depth in the chapters followed, but they help to give a snapshot of the key strategic areas for the city in the second decade of the twenty first century.

Information Technology, Innovation, Research and Development

When fifty of the world's top academics were asked what they thought critical in addressing the world's problems in the coming half century, all said that Education was the key priority. Investment in the infrastructure of education and in delivery of different forms of training has also been one of the key areas of co-operation between enterprises and government. For the UK, for instance, it currently commits 6.1 per cent of its GDP to education. Across the EU it is 5.3% per cent. In the US, it is 6.12 per cent. In China, it is 0.54 per cent. In the US, 70 per cent of students now go from high school to some form of tertiary level education. In the UK, from the period 1997 to 2008, the level rose from 20 per cent to 45 per cent. It is clear that in the battle for competitiveness, and to create good value jobs, that fulfil the expectations of an increasingly demanding population, education is key. China currently has only 2 per cent of its population going to tertiary level institutes. Even so, in the last three decades, over one million Chinese have studied abroad. This marks a major investment in training. Universities like Fudan and Jiaotong and Tongji in Shanghai are involved in the strategy to create world class training institutes.

Education and training lie at the heart of travelling towards what academic Hu Chuanli in his annual reports about China's project of modernising from the Chinese Academy of Sciences in China's calls 'China's post industrial modernity.' The partnership between business and education works in a number of ways – both to create stronger research and development, but also to build stronger vocational training, and to focus on the economic impact of research. Corporations also become increasingly important sources of funding for education and research.

With this strand goes information technology. In 2000, in the EU, less than 5 per cent of business was done online. Now it has increased to 25 per cent. Its increase has created new ways of doing business, new ways of engaging with clients and customers, and also new business models. Information technology has advanced more quickly than many expected. It has also made some areas of business defunct, and created others. Information technology has created a different meaning for the customer, and for the role of enterprise, and entrepreneurial activity. China's potential here is obvious. In 1998, only 2 per cent of Chinese nationally were connected to the internet. Now the number of net users has risen to over 900 million, the largest in any country in the world. Their internet habits are markedly different to those in developed country markets, with more usage of mobile devices, less reliance on credit card payments, more preselection of goods and then visiting purchase centres to look at them and then actually buy. Even so, credit card usage in China has risen rapidly, and we expect to see the same levels of internet retailing as in other markets soon. The Five Year Programme talks of 'developing e-business actively, improving e-business services orientated to SMEs,' and 'promoting the construction of society-orientated credit services, online payment and logistic distribution.' This will be looked at in more detail in the sections on government service and also retail later.

China, through companies like Baidu and Alibaba, has been an innovator in this area. However, the Five Year Programme spells out a deeper engagement with innovation, and this is backed up by statements from former Party Secretary and President Hu Jintao in his speech at the 17th Party Congress in 2007, in which he talked of the need to create an innovative culture, one that was willing to allow more space for experimentation and adaptation. Innovation is one of the most frequently used words in the national and municipal Five Year Programme. It talks of an 'innovation driven' strategy of 'reinvigorating the country through human resource development' and through 'technological innovation.' It talks of 'innovating the provision of methods of public service', and 'innovating in the mechanisms of social management.' This stress on innovation indicates that China has a high awareness of the challenges as it undertakes a transition from an industrialising, export directed economic model, to one where there are now as many as 100 million who might be considered members of the professional middle class, and whose expectations of government and corporate behaviour are very high. Innovation's role is to attempt to follow the rapid economic and social changes, creating new ways of doing things which are more effective, but not disruptive. But we need to think very hard about the meaning of innovation, and how best to create a benign environment for the kinds of innovation that are fruitful. Innovation also means an acceptance of experimentation, and of the often high failure rate of attempts at change and modification.

Figures on research and development in the early 2000s, before China entered the World Trade Organisation (WTO) showed that spending by corporations on research and development was very low in China compared to the US and EU. According to Professor Peter Nolan of Cambridge University, in the late 1990 and early 2000s, Chinese state and non state enterprises committed less than 1 per cent of their turnover to investment in research and development.[13] In the last few years, however, under the last programme and this, that has increased. Productive spending on research and development is one of the most important drivers for modernisation and innovation. But it is absolutely essential that money spent on research and development, especially government money channelled through universities and research institutes, is properly directed and has clear relevance to the productive sectors of the economy. Universities have enormous pools of talent on which both government and corporations can profitably draw, but simple increases in research funding, while admirable and worthwhile, are not of themselves sufficient to ensure that the resources are used productively. Explicit goals and outcomes need to be established from the start with clear lines of accountability. Chinese state and non state companies and the foreign companies have long been close partners in research and there are rich institutional links at all levels in the educational sector: schools, vocational colleges and universities.

Corporations and governments are key partners in research and development. The policy framework for enabling this needs to be utterly clear. What incentives are there for the support of R and D, and what role do MNCs play for this in China and in Shanghai? This is an area that needs detailed policies and regulations. Shanghai has already recognised the centrality of R and D for supporting economic development and fulfilling its ambitious developmental plans. Innovation and creativity run as major themes throughout

---

13. Peter Nolan. *China in the Global Economy*. Palgrave, 2001.

the five year programme – it is in new strategic industries, new technologies, greener and more efficient technologies that much of Shanghai's future effort will be placed. These will demand a steady stream of new ideas and innovative practices. Unless corporations can be confident that Shanghai can provide a suitable and conducive environment for research and development, they will prefer to conduct it elsewhere. A key issue here will remain intellectual property protection, which continues to be a concern for many foreign corporations and increasingly for Chinese corporations as they put more money and effort into research and technology. Part of the answer obviously lies with national level regulation, but equally important will be the general business environment that Shanghai municipality provides. This will include legislation and reliable means of enforcement of that legislation which are seen as fair and accessible to all, but it also includes a generating wider measure of trust in the general operating environment – clarity and an open and accessible legal system are the basic building blocks here. There is much to be done in this area and considerable room for both exchanges of ideas between business and government and more formal interactions.

Sustainability

The Five Year Programme is rich in references to the sustainability and climate change agenda. 'We will positively respond to global climate change,' it states. 'Massive reductions in energy consumption intensity should be regarded as binding.' This is backed up by the target adopted in 2009 after the Copenhagen Climate Change summit of reducing greenhouse gases by up to 45 per cent compared to 2005 levels by 2020. [14] The plan also talks of strengthening international exchange and strategic policy dialogue in this area, and developing pragmatic co-operation in areas like scientific research, technology research and development and capacity building. In fact the link between this and the agenda covered above of innovation, research and development and education is very clear.

---

14. *International Institutional Investor*, 2010(4), pp.34–35.

Enterprises in China have been estimated to produce over a quarter of the country's greenhouse gas emissions. So the role of corporations is very important. China has exacting targets for emissions at both national and local level, and China has been at the forefront of developing new and greener technologies. The change in the industrial structure in Shanghai will no doubt contribute to the ability to achieve the new targets on emissions as older, less efficient industries give way to newer more energy efficient ones.

Delivering on the green agenda is crucial not just for the image of a company, but also for its competitiveness. It is now rightly a fundamental of its business model. Here, the role of government in creating the right policies and supportive environment is critical. The 12th Five Year Programme talks in detail about objectives for supporting the green agenda, from improving water to restoring the environmental health to rivers and lakes. The link with enterprise and innovation is also made. Incentives need to be given to allow companies to experiment and contribute in this area. In the areas of circular uses of resources and enhancing the recycling system, companies like Tesco and those in the retailing sector have a critical function in partnering government. But the key thing is to have clarity in regulations and laws to show how this is done. This is also intimately linked to the other important strand in the programme – improvements in people's wellbeing.

Internationalisation

In the last few years, Shanghai has had a specific objective of developing an international financial centre. The 12th Five Year Programme specifically mentions the Shanghai Pudong New

Area. Established when former Premier Zhu Rongji was Mayor of Shanghai in the early 1990s, Pudong has become one of the fastest growing development areas in the world. Shanghai is the key location for the Chinese authorities as they move forward with their plans to allow stronger commercial law. The city's aspirations to be a major international financial centre has been repeated a number of times over the last few years. Dr. Fang Xinghai, Director General of the city's Financial Services Office, in an interview in April 2010 for International Finance Magazine, stated that 'the State Council directive is mainly to speed up Shanghai's transformation... Shanghai will be among the top three [financial centres] in the world as early as 2015.'[15] Dr Fang continued: 'We don't want to make an international financial centre for the sake of being an international finance centre. We want it to serve the interests of the people.'

One of the primary objectives of the opening up of China to foreign inward investment in the 1980s was not so much to attract capital, as to also gain know how and technology. We can also see this in some of the investments that are being made out of China in the last few years. China saw itself as lacking technology, and management expertise, and so it set up provincial and national policies, many of them driven through the special economic zones, which supported attracting companies to invest in China that brought in these two assets.

After over a quarter of a century, this requirement and the policies supporting it are inevitably much more sophisticated. In the period from 1980 to 2011, cities like Shanghai have seen the creation of a new professional middle class, and of entrepreneurs. They are at the heart of new consumption patterns we see emerging in China, and have been integral to the process of urbanisation and the rising expectations from people from both corporate and government services. The Five Year Programme talks of the need to improve 'scientific decision making', and of strengthening 'the restructuring

---

15. Interview in *International Institutional Investor*, April 2010, pp.34-35.

of government performance assessment and administrative accountability.' In many areas of their lives, the emerging Chinese middle class, those with a per capita GDP of over USD10 thousand per annum, are demanding new levels of management and of service, and excellence in terms of quality of goods. The Programme's discussion of the need to create brands partially addresses this. Consumer movements have been important in addressing quality standards in food, manufactured goods, and appliances.

Chinese manufacturers are also aspiring to produce more own-branded goods which supply quality products. They too see the huge opportunities in the domestic market, with new, discerning consumers. In the early to middle periods of Chinese economic modernism, therefore, foreign brands were seen as largely trustworthy, and as enjoying an advantage over local brands. For many local brands, the key strategy was to create partnerships where they could leverage off association with an international brand, and then create goods for the local and international market with some of the know how and management input from these partnerships.

In fact, we see in the last decade, a gradual but accelerating shift. We know that many hi-tech and high value goods are in fact made in China. Ipods and Iphones are largely manufactured in the Pearl River Delta. Many household appliances are made in Chinese factories. The relationship between foreign and Chinese partners has matured and become more sophisticated. We are now seeing mutual learning, rather than learning going one way. We are also seeing foreign companies who wish to penetrate the Chinese market that is emerging and becoming more important needing to work more deeply with local partners to understand the dynamics of the indigenous market.

The Five Year Programme talks about innovation a great deal. One of the areas of innovation that relates to the interface between foreign and local businesses is in the changes in financial services, in local business regulations, and in financial innovation. Here Shanghai occupies a critical place. In the last few years, it has looked closely at creating a market for RMB business. It is also looking more closely at areas like actively participating in global economic governance and regional co-operation, at developing overseas investment co-operation, signing mutual agreements on investment protection and on measures to avoid double taxation. In the five year programme it talks of 'continuing the combination of the strategies of "bringing in" and "going out",' paying 'equal attention to both foreign investments in China and Chinese investments abroad.' This is 'in order to increase sage and effective use of the two markets and resources.' Shanghai will be key to China's overall success in this endeavour. It already has a strong foundation in its growing financial system and financial services market. But equally important will be robust supervisory and regulatory systems to control and prevent the occasional excesses to which the financial sector can be prone. China's financial system escaped the immediate impact of the global financial crisis. But it is not immune from future shocks of its own. China is already experiencing problems with an overblown housing market that is showing many of the characteristics of a traditional financial bubble. There are concerns being voiced about the extent of local government debt in China and the impact this may have on the overall financial system.

One of the important objectives prefigured in the Programme is the creation of a more robust financial services sector within China. It is estimated that as China moves towards middle income status, and sees the maturing of its internal market, just as in Europe or the US, there will be a sharp increase in financial services for consumers, and an increase in the jobs created in this sector. China has now opened up areas like education, medicine and sports to international partners, attempting to improve the international level of the service sector. In the UK, the service sector makes up 77 per cent of GDP. In China at the moment this is 43 per cent. [16] There is a plan to increase this to over 60 per cent by 2025. And Shanghai is very much at the forefront of this process, aiming to achieve 65 per cent of GDP

---

16. Source: CIA Yearbook, https://www.cia.gov/library/publications/the-world-factbook/geos/ch.html

in the service industries by 2015. What happens in Shanghai and how it manages this transition will be closely watched by the central leadership as they try to move other areas of China into a more developed phase. Developed countries, and particularly the UK which is now very heavily dependent on the services sector, have already made this transition. It is in this area that new forms of partnership are most likely between foreign entities and Chinese partners.

Conclusion

This chapter has set out the context of Shanghai's development through the genesis of previous city plans over the last nine decades, the relationship between these and national development plans in the Five Year Programmes, and the ways in which Pudong area has been one of the great experiments in development and modernisation undertaken within any city in modern China.

It is noticeable though that much of the language used in the documents looked at in this chapter is highly aspirational and general. The question as the city goes more deeply into the 21st century is in what ways it can specifically meet the new challenges being presented it through deeper globalisation, higher social mobility, and greater complexity in the local and national economies. In 1999 the city set itself a broad strategic objective by 2020, just as the country did. But the issues now as it had travelled halfway along this path are more about detailed areas of implementation and policy rather than restatements of these grand objectives. The rest of this book will therefore look at very specific areas and state where these stand at present, and where they are likely to be in the coming decade.

Annex

A Tale of Two Cities: Shanghai and Beijing

Shanghai and Beijing both occupy uniquely important roles both in Chinese history, in the political geography of the country, and in its contemporary economy. Some might see this as a highly competitive relationship, where Beijing as the seat of national government enjoys the same privileged space as other capital cities and is able to control and micro manage developments in Shanghai. There has been historic distrust and strong cultural differences between both places.

In a World Bank comparative study of the two cities issued in 2010, economists Shahid Yusuf and Kaoru Nabeshima place the advantages and drawbacks of each city beside each other. Their starting point is simple recognition that Beijing, accounting in 2009 for 4 per cent of national GDP, and Shanghai, accounting for 5 per cent, occupy uniquely import positions in the domestic economy. They then draw on the two cities capacities in terms of education, innovation, industrial structure in order to map out how they relate to each other. 'To realise their longer-run objectives', they state of the two cities:

'[they] will need to pursue strategies that fully reflect their acquired comparative advantages and their current industrial mix as well as the opportunities for growth, local employment and trade offered by the various activities that either city could develop. Although an overlap between the activities conducive to rapid growth is inevitable, the trajectories followed by Beijing and Shanghai to date and the economic composition of the two cities also recommend a differentiation of future strategies and, necessarily, a differentiation of objectives.'[17]

---

17. Shahid Yusuf; Kaoru Nabeshima. *Two Dragon Heads: Contrasting Development Paths for Beijing and Shanghai*. The World Bank/International Bank for Reconstruction and Development, Washington, 2010, pp.2–3.

For both cities, they see a common challenge which 'is to embed a culture of innovation that both nurtures existing growth industries and stimulates desirable creative destruction by inducing new activities that could be tomorrow's lead sectors.' [18] And for both they see the need for a 'multi sectoral strategy', with Beijing concentrating on hi tech and high value added industry, and Shanghai on commerce and manufacturing. Their position is that 'most industrial cities are unable to make a transition to global cities led by finance and other business services alone.' [19]

But their conclusion is a simple 'yes' as to whether Shanghai and Beijing can co-exist and mutually complement each other:

'Because the evolution of these two cities has proceeded down different paths, as is reflected in their economic structure and industrial mix, and the experiences that they have accumulated differ, their future development paths will not be the same. Instead, these two cities will develop somewhat differently, taking advantage of their individual experiences, complementing each other.'

---

18. Ibid., p.4.
19. Ibid., p.63.

Chapter Three

Shanghai and Globalisation: The 2010 Expo

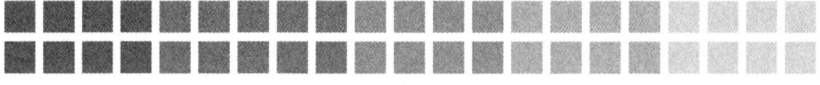

Historically, right from the 19th century, Shanghai has seen itself as a global city. This is vividly illustrated by the links illustrated in the first chapter between the buildings lining the Bund and the foreign companies, architects, owners and residents connected with them, from the time they were built (in some cases over a century ago) till now. The tradition of close links between Shanghai and the rest of the world continues today with the diverse international environment that now exists in Pudong and Puxi. In the plans outlined in the last chapter, there is a recurrence of this issue of the city's global role, usually as a key priority. This chapter will look at the role that international events, and in particular the Shanghai 2010 Expo, played in both the globalization agenda of the city, and in its development of its own internal strategic priorities.

The Shanghai Expo is a useful case study. An immense event, held over six months in 2010, it saw nearly 80 million visitors come to the huge Expo site, over 98 per cent of them from within China. For almost every day, half a million people visited the various pavilions, showcasing different parts of the world. This international face of the Expo was something well covered in reports. The BBC reported on 29 April 2010 that 'Shanghai Expo is China's New Showcase to the World.' Hosting the event, the report stated, was an opportunity to 'show the millions of Chinese that will visit the Expo just how important and influential their country has become.'[1]

For several years before the Expo, I was aware of its importance to Chinese people, and in particular to Shanghai. In 2001 and 2002, while a diplomat in Beijing at the British Embassy, I remember the question of how the UK should support China's bid to hold the event, and the early commitments we gave to having stand. This was unusual. Governments usually allowed companies or the non state sector to be involved in these sort of events. To participate as a government in the first place was unusual, but there was a sense that this would be an Expo unlike any other and in that sense merited an exception being made. Part of this was also from a calculation of self interest. The UK like most other developed economies were aware once China had entered the World Trade Organisation in 2001 of how its domestic market was likely to grow and open up even more. An event like this at least gave one opportunity to showcase British manufacturing excellence and technology before a big new audience.

The road from 2002 when Shanghai secured the Expo to 2010, when the event finally opened, was a tough one. In 2008 the global financial crisis meant that the UK, like most other participants from the developing world, had to revise its budget, and look for involvement by foreign donors. One of the most important was BP, the petroleum company. A number of others contributed, either in cash or in materials or help. There was a wide understanding that even with tightened budgets, the UK still needed to take this chance to showcase itself to the world's largest source of new potential consumers.

By 2008 I was an advisor to the Liverpool City Government, directing the Liverpool Shanghai Partnership, which was a body supported by universities, local government, and companies across the City. Liverpool itself had links with Shanghai going back deep into the 19th century, and boasted Europe's earliest Chinatown. It

---

1. Hogg, BBC website

was natural therefore that in 2007 the city should make a bid for one of the stands in the Urban Best Practice area of the Expo, along with most of Shanghai's other sister cities across the globe. The heart of this bid was the stress on Shanghai and Liverpool having something beyond logistic links in common with each other. They were both wrestling with the challenges of preserving their historic fabric while also fulfilling the needs of a dynamic modern economy. Liverpool in its dock area was proud of the fact that it had been accorded World Heritage Site Status by the UN Education, Science and Culture Organisation (UNESCO), something that figured as the heart of its bid to a stand in the Shanghai EXPO where it wished to showcase its own experiences of preservation with renovation.

The challenge for Liverpool, having won the bid, of holding what was in effect a six month long exhibition at the other side of the world was something that dawned on the people I was advising even as they were still celebrating winning their selection bid. Consultants were employed to draw up blue prints of what the stand would look like, plans were made about how to staff it, and proposals for what major events to hold over the period of the EXPO. There was never any doubt that this was a major opportunity for Liverpool in building deeper links with Shanghai, not that there was a major need to make this an advert for what the city had to offer to not just Shanghainese, but also Chinese tourists, students and business people. It was these three who were presented as the major targets of the campaign.

What was clear in all the research we did in the long build up to the Expo was that Liverpool had two major assets which all Chinese knew – the two football clubs it was home to, and the fact it was also the birthplace of the Beatles. These therefore were central to the whole marketing strategy. But there was also a lot of work on how to present a story of the other, lesser well known aspects of Liverpool in a way that might be attractive to visitors wandering around the EXPO. Music as supplied through the Royal Philharmonic Orchestra, the oldest in the UK. Images of the famous waterfront were put up on screens, with displays of Shanghai's Bund beside them to show similarities. Some idea of the other cultural assets of the city were displayed, from its major museums, its art galleries and its two cathedrals.

One of the more extraordinary aspects of the EXPO, however, to me as someone observing this intensification of the relationship between the two cities over this period, was simply how much the participants from Liverpool were also learning about the city they were now visiting and engaging with through work on this stand. I was present when a number of delegations went to Shanghai, and was always struck by the ways in which people fell silent when they first saw the Bund and the waterfront along the Huangpu River, absorbing the astonishing site of the river crammed with boats, and the buildings ranged opposite with their variety and grandeur. It was at moments like this that the relationship between Liverpool and Shanghai became transformation and real, and actually entered into people's lives, rather than existing as something abstract and purely symbolic.

Expos in General

Expos have an intimate link with the development of the industrial revolution, and date back to the middle of the 19th century. The first proper Expo was held in Crystal Palace, London, in 1851. Strongly supported by the consort of Queen Victoria, Prince Albert, it symbolized the new confidence and influence of a Britain that was the first to have engaged with the processes of industrialization and which was at the forefront then of ideas of progress and development. In the subsequent century and a half of Expos, they have been used to promote notions of industrialization, to support cultural exchange, and to brand nations. In particular they have assisted in their soft power diplomacy. Modern Expos are governed by the 1928 Convention Relating to International Exhibitions, with the Bureau International des Expositions (International Exhibition Bureau) serving as the main authorized body. In recent years, the main Expos (there are other, smaller scale specialized events) are held every five years.

Shanghai had long had an interest in hosting a major international event, with Liang Qichao, one of the great modernizing intellectuals from the Qing dynasty being an early proponent. Shanghai Municipal Government had shown interest in having the Expo in the 1980s, but in view of the fact that reform had just started then, the timing was regarded as inappropriate. The city started gathering support for its first earnest bid as early as 2001. At the 132nd meeting of the Bureau of International Expositions held in Monaco, Monte Carlo, on the 3 December 2002, Shanghai competed against Yeosu in South Korea, Moscow in the Russian Federation, Queretaro in Mexico and Wroclaw in Poland. It came top of the bidding for each of the four rounds of voting with the delegates, and was declared the winner.

One of the first questions raised once the nomination was secured was how the site selected for the location for the event should be planned and prepared. A site divided by the Huangpu River was selected, covering over 5.28 kms. The theme of the Expo was 'Better City Better Life,' and the duration to be from May 1st to October 31st 2010.

Preparation for an event which aimed to have over 200 countries participating and 70 million people attend was always going to be challenging. In the eight years of planning, over USD 48 billion was spent, with large parts of the city reconstructed. The Expo had a dual face. On the one hand, as the BBC report stated, it was a chance for China and the city to showcase itself to the world. But it was also an event which could be used to achieve some of the city's own strategic developmental objectives. These two aspects will be looked at in assessing how the Expo went. As the Liverpool delegation mentioned

Shanghai 2020

above also showed, it was an opportunity too for the world to get to know more about Shanghai.

The World in One City for Six Months

The size of the Expo meant that during planning it was decided to have five zones. The first three of these, Zones A, B and C, were south of the Huangpu River on the Pudong side, and the final two, D and E, North in the Puxi area. In Zone A stood the massive Chinese pavilion, with its distinctive red, V shaped design, dominating the central area of the Expo site. This zone also had China's provincial pavilions, and those from other Asian countries. In Zone B stood the national pavilions of countries like Australia, Cambodia and Indonesia, along with the pavilions for international organizations from ASEAN to the World Wildlife Fund and the United Nations. In Zone C, the African pavilions stood alongside Caribbean, European and Central and South American countries. Across the river in Zone D there were company pavilions, from Coca Cola to the State Grid and CISCO, and in Zone E Urban Best Practice Pavilions, some from Shanghai's 66 sister cities.

The final tally for attendance at the Expo was 190 countries with a presence, and 73.08 million attendees.

Volunteering and the Expo

One of the key elements of hosting the 2010 Expo was to encourage volunteering. For this, an Expo Volunteer Department was established in June 2007. From 2009, the Expo organisers started looking for volunteers. Over 620 thousand applications were received, with 90,000 finally selected. Over 95 per cent of these were under 30 years of age, with the oldest being 74. The majority of volunteers did two weeks, with only 200 in charge of management and volunteering for a longer period. Their work included giving out information to attendees at the Expo, showing visitors around, cleaning up public spaces, and helping with logistics. About 200 were from overseas, the majority from Japan and Hong Kong. [2]

Volunteering is a relatively new concept in China. But there is a strong tradition of offering help within communities both in rural and urban China. This builds naturally into international concepts of people giving up their time for socially helpful work rather than remuneration. Two volunteers interviewed in November 2012 on their experiences of the Expo were positive about the ways in which it had helped them appreciate the value of volunteering. One of them, a man in his sixties who had been born and brought up in Shanghai and lived there all his life. He had been an engineer before retirement. His experience of the Expo had taught him about how his native city had become more open as a result of hosting the event. He felt that during the event, the city residents had shown that they could be immensely hospitable. In his personal life, this had also helped him in relating to people from a younger generation. The other, a younger woman originally from the north east of China had come to the city to study and decided to volunteer in order to get a wider social network and understand her

---

2. Interview, Shanghai, August 2010

adopted city better. Despite the long periods in which people needed to be on duty, from 5 in the morning to 5 at night, or 5 at night till 11, and the very hot temperatures in which people had had to work, she still felt that participating in the event in this way had been worthwhile. One particular event had had an impact on her – the final day, in late October, when over a million visitors had come to the site. Meeting these challenges meant that everyone, in their various teams, had to think up ways of ensuring that problems were avoided, or solved once they had arisen. In particular, they had found ways to entertain people when they were queuing, some of them for many hours, to see some of the stands.

■■■■■■■■■■■■■■■■■■■■■■■■■■

According to officials, there were a number of aims for the Expo:

- It had to be the best attended in the history of international general expositions.
- It had to attract enterprises from abroad to attend.
- The attendance of Taiwan was also important
- To make the spectacle experience of those attending valuable and special. In particular, the quality of the stands was considered a priority.
- To avoid any major security incidents. [3]

In fact, the Urban Development Plan from 2006, covering the Five Year Period during which the Expo was due to be held, was explicit in what the aims for the city were in holding the Expo:

> *'Hosting Expo 2010 successfully is an important move to implement national strategy and raise the*

---

3. Interview with Municipal Government official, Shanghai, November 2012

international profile of the city. To stage a successful
world Exposition, the city should hasten to build up and
improve its infrastructure system, including functional
hubs and networks, to improve the quality of municipal
administration in an all-round way, to strengthen its
urban civilization, most notable the civility of its citizens.
Expo 2010 should be utilized as a platform to improve
the city's international communications abilities, to
promote harmony between rural and urban development,
to promote mutual development between Shanghai and
other areas in the Yangtze River Delta and to achieve
interactive development between Shanghai and the central
and western regions of China.'* [4]*

Expo Assessment

Officials talked of the Expo before it was held as the fulfillment of a 'hundred year dream', and indeed during the Expo itself the Expo news department released information stating that there had been Chinese participation in the earliest 1851 London Expo. According to one official, China wanted the Expo 'for the world to understand China and for China to understand the world.' [5] There were plenty of challenges that had been foreseen in 2002 when the nomination was secured in Monte Carlo. The scale of the planned event marked it out as different from those that had been run before. Aichi in Japan, where the 2005 Expo was held, had less than 25 million visitors.

---

4. Chapter Four of the *City Development Plan for the 11th Five Year Programme Period*. p.167.
5. Interview, Shanghai, November 2012

Milan, where the next Expo will be held in 2015, is planning only a quarter of the visitors Shanghai aimed for. Because of this difference in scale, as one official in the Shanghai World Expo Corporation who had been intimately involved in the planning of the event up to 2010 said in November 2012, new ways of thinking had to be introduced. From 2002, there were five year preparatory plans, and a number of innovations, with temporary buildings and roads constructed to set in place the infrastructure to hold the event. There were plenty of unforeseen issues.

The most significant of these unplanned challenges happened from 2008. While most countries were highly supportive of Shanghai's hosting of the event, the impact of the global financial crisis from late 2008 onwards meant many had to revise their participation strategy. Iceland, because of its crisis from the collapse of its banks, temporarily had to withdraw. Many countries which had been expecting much heavier corporate support had to scale back their plans or rethink their funding strategy. One issue that helped countries and participants maintain commitment was that the sustainability theme of the Expo which proved a timely and popular one. For the US, therefore, while the government had initially not supported the Expo, the theme made it more sympathetic. Attendance at the Expo was seen as a good investment, despite initial skepticism.

The Expo was seen in assessments after the event had closed in October as a great victory for collaboration, with seven to eight thousand people working each day on hosting the visitors, sometimes in extremely hot and difficult weather. In a meeting hosted by the Municipal Government in 2012 to carry out an overall assessment, a number of issues were discussed. The city government had been wary of hosting such a massive event with limited experience, but was pleased with the way in which the whole event progressed. They recognized the importance of partnership, and in particular the help of the Ministry of Foreign Affairs, the Ministry of Foreign Commerce, and other national ministries. This showed how barriers could come down and people and institutions at national and local could work together for a common purpose. The assessments about the way in which as a society the city unified, with different kinds of volunteers involved, was also positive. This unity was also manifested through the hosting of people from throughout China, and the sense of community as Shanghainese tolerated both the inconvenience before when infrastructure was being put in place and then the challenge of the event itself as it was held from May onwards.

In terms of the strategic objectives set out above, most were considered to have been achieved. The Expo attracted 246 enterprises from overseas to exhibit, Taiwan took a pavilion, and the opening and closing ceremonies were considered a success. The quality of the stands was regarded, amongst independent assessors, to be very high, with particularly strong marks going to the Saudi Arabian stand (which, at some points in the Expo, had nine hour queues to go in). Over 30 received prizes. There were also no major security incidents.

In less easily measurable areas, the meeting also judged that the event had met its objectives. In particular, it had:

- Made Shanghai more open to reform. The Expo showed openness, and helped to change the habits of Shanghainese, in terms of teaching many to care for the environment, clear rubbish up even when it was not directly around their places of work or residence, educating them about volunteering and the value of giving their time for work in society without remuneration.
- Improved the sense of service delivery and co-ordination, particularly from government agencies and community groups. The hosting of the Expo set out international standards against which the city could try to benchmark itself.
- Improved notions of service quality, so that the idea of 'taking people as the key' was moved from a rhetorical statement to something that people could actually see happening. The vast nature of the Expo meant that the government had to

consult widely, communicate its objectives, explain why the inconvenience which happened before the Expo was necessary, and show leadership.

- Improved the city's waste management practices. The sheer numbers of those coming to the event meant that there were huge challenges of dealing with waste management. Part of this was simply educating people to be conscious of handling their own waste and putting it in bins rather than simply chucking it on the floor.

In that sense, as the official said, the Expo was 'a laboratory' for the whole of the city and its management practices, in which it was able to try out new ideas.

Beyond all of this, the primary educational objective of the Expo was to teach a huge number of people about the objectives of environmentalism. It did this through illustrating best practices from other places across the globe, but also through showing the many tens of millions of Chinese that came ways in which, in their daily lives, they could contribute to preserving the environment. For that reason, as the official stated, 'while the Expo taught Shanghai how to hold international conferences, the main achievement was in people's consciousness.'

The Sustainable Use of the Expo Site

One of the legacies of the Expo 2010 is the use of the actual site, one which spreads over an area twice the size of Monaco and which had undergone extensive cleansing and decontamination work before being used. During the Expo, over half a million people had come onto the site each day, creating huge logistic challenges. The end of the Expo, however, did not mean that the site was to fall back into neglect. Part of the rationale for holding the event was to find ways of regenerating this area just as other parts of Pudong had been regenerated in the early 1990s. In order to achieve it, the Shanghai World Expo Group was set up, with some government funding and secondments by officials into the company, to take charge of the commercial redevelopment of the site. This company is to eventually be self funding, after government capital investment. Current revenues come from renting out parts of the site, and the use of land.

In 2012, the main focal area for redevelopment is the larger Pudong side of the site. In the central Zone A, four buildings had been left over from the Expo to be maintained in use.

- The Mercedes Building
- The China Pavilion, which still hosts a museum and which has 10,000 visitors a day in 2012
- The commercial centre
- The Shanghai Meeting Centre, which hosts government and commercial meetings

The first phase of the redevelopment plan for the Expo site beyond these already extent buildings will be the creation in the central entry place running through the heart of the Pudong site of a shopping mall, to be in place by the end of 2013.[6]

In terms of new buildings, the following are planned:

- Four new hotels by 2015-2016

---

6. Interview, Shanghai, November 2012

- 60 thousand square metres for enterprises next to the commercial centre
- 92 thousand square meters in the east of Pudong for commercial use
- A further hotel district

In order to achieve this commercial and residential use, the Shanghai World Expo Group has planned new transport to service the area, new tunnels, two new bridges, and three new lines for the underground, with the 8th line opening in December 2012. For the building of skyscrapers, learning from Pudong there is a plan to phase the size of these, with smaller at the front near the water's edge, and taller ones further inland. Roads are intended to be less wide and with more frequent stops so that they are more pedestrian friendly. Parking will go underground, as is the energy infrastructure. The objective is to make the area a greener environment. The Expo area here is planned, in the next decade, to be a centre for enterprises as well as residential use, somewhere that exemplifies mixed use, rather than being one or the other. In that sense, it will act as a home to innovative, modern enterprises and give them the kinds of infrastructure and links into the community where there can be more organic urban commercial and living growth.

For the Puxi side of the Expo, covering what had been Zones D and E, the emphasis will be on creating a cultural city, with an international standard museum. This underlines the aspirations for Shanghai as a whole to become a major tourist destination. Models of good city practice will be placed in the museum. In what had been the Expo village, which had contained the administrative and staff blocks during the event itself, local government will take up residence.

One of the ambitions in the redevelopment would be to exploit the river, rather than to obscure or ignore it. The Huangpu River is an integral part of the cityscape, so has to be incorporated in any plans.

What Is Worth It?

The cost of the Expo leading up to the event's opening had been a constant issue for media interest, just as the Beijing Olympics in 2008. The immense cost of the event was often mentioned, along with the rebuilding of parts of the city. These issues of cost did not go away. Blogger Han Han, who has over 2 million users on the Sina Weibo site he runs, was one of the most vocal. Speaking of the whole concept of an Expo, he wrote: 'Imagine a domestic clothing brand with an excellent advertising campaign whose clothes you wear, feeling hip and totally connected. Then you go abroad and notice that in fact you're wearing a brand that's not at all fashionable, that's outdated.' Another reported students in Beijing University stating that 'China would be much better to invest all the billions in education and medical care.' [7] Another critic on the Global Times website complained that 'Chinese volunteers and Pavilion workers do not have the desired quality. While visiting Saudi, I saw one volunteer allow a foreign (sic) to jump the queue.' [8] There were, of course, initial teething problems. According to one report, visitor numbers for the first three days of the event were far lower than had been expected. 'Some 70 million visitors – mostly Chinese – are expected to visit the enormous site over the next six months when the fair is open. But to achieve this, more than 380,000 people need to visit each day. So far, the highest number each day has been about 215,000,' wrote Chris Hogg of the BBC website on the 3rd May. One report in the British Guardian stated that the Expo was 'set to be the world's most expensive party.' [9]

One of the greatest problems is that during the construction period of the site, traffic was disrupted, and large parts of the centre of the city were affected by the building of train and underground

---

7. www.swissinfo.ch, 11 May 2010
8. *Global Times* opinion pages, posted by Au-Tree, 17 May 2010
9. *Guardian*, 21 April 2010

lines, new roads and tunnel systems. For over a year the front of the Bund was obscured by works as a new lay out was constructed. From 2007, six new subway lines were opened, including lines 6, 7, 8, 9, 10, 11, with line 22 opened in 2012. The construction of the fastest growing metro system in the world, however, has proved to be a good investment. According to one long term foreign resident interviewed in November 2012, Shanghai had managed to build over a decade's worth of infrastructure in the space of four years. The impact of this on the city's environment and traffic problems has been considerable. This will be looked at in the chapter on sustainability.

For the criticisms made over the expense of hosting the Expo and the disruption, therefore, there were other voices who applauded the emphasis being given to sustainability and to greening the city, with the huge efforts being put into educating the population about the importance of these issues. Christian Gurtler, president of the Swiss Chinese Chamber of Commerce, stated in May 2010 that the Expo was 'the first time for about 80 years that a world exhibition has gone for concrete issues.' Nicolas Musy, a Swiss businessman, went further, saying 'There is a pragmatic side to the Chinese which leads them to take advantage of the Expo to think about what a model town in China should be like. Another aim of the Expo is to define the quality of life in Shanghai for the future.'[10] In that sense, hosting the event did have strategic objectives, which were in line with those spelt out in the 1999-2020 Urban Plan and in the Five Year Programmes.

Shanghai Disneyland

While the Expo was an event limited in duration, which had to have

---

10. www.swissinfo.ch, 11 May 2010

an impact over the six months during which it was held, the planned Disneyland, due to open in 2015, will be permanent. Following on from the smaller resort built in Hong Kong Special Administrative Region (SAR) and opened in 2005, the Shanghai resort will be the first within Mainland China, and is being built as part of a joint venture between the Walt Disney Company and the Shanghai Shendi Group. It was approved by the central government in 2009, with a total investment of RMB 24 billion. Groundbreaking began in April 2011, with a planned area of four square kilometers, in the southeast of Pudong.

According to the Disney Resorts website, the concept of the park will be simple: 'With Shanghai Disneyland, guests of all ages will have an exciting and extraordinary new place to play. Shanghai will include signature Disney experiences that guests around the world know and love, but will also feature exciting new elements that will be unique to the Shanghai Disney Resort. Shanghai,' it concludes, 'will be both authentically Disney and distinctly Chinese.'

One of the legacies of the Expo that the Park is already encouraging is volunteering. On December 5th 2012, on International Volunteer Day (which also coincides with the anniversary of Walt Disney's birthday) a report issued by the resort stated that 'Shanghai Disney resort partnered with Chuansha New Town People's Government and Habitat for Humanity to organize a "school beatification programme" ... event.' Howard Brown, Project Development Executive of the resort stated that 'our Imagineers are excited to use their artistic experience and skills to assist students in beautifying their own campus and inspire learning and creativity and a greater awareness of volunteerism.'[11]

Disney of course is an iconic brand, and one that has great traction particularly in Asia. In that sense, opening one of the few approved resorts outside America in Shanghai is an accolade. But there are

---

11. Shanghai Disney Resort website, www.en.shanghaisneyresort.com.cn

more probing voices who are critical of the very American nature of Sydney, and how it promotes US soft power but has little real resonance with Chinese culture. Similar criticisms greeted the opening of the EuroDisney resort in the early 1990s, where French critics complained about the creation of a 'Mickey Mouse culture.' In many ways, the bolder aspiration for Shanghai would be to devise their own indigenous theme park, but that is linked with the creation of national soft power images.

International Events

In 2008, I was the guest of a company supporting the Shanghai Formula One race in the city. Attending it was an interesting experience. I remember the lobbying and support that the British government had given the organizers of the Formula One race earlier in the decade, when places as far and wide as Xi'an and Beijing had been suggested as possible locations. Building a race track sounds easy, but in fact is a massive and costly investment. There are few places with the infrastructure, the open space and the ability to host an event like this. And because it is an annual event, there have to be other uses for the race track when the competition is not taking place. Going on the busses from the hotel to the race track far out from the city centre, I was struck by just how much of a challenge getting the race track completed must have been – a huge area, with viewing platforms, corporate boxes and paddocks, the noise of the racing cars simply overwhelming as they sped by.

Hosting event like the F1 is important for the globalization of Shanghai partly because of their usefulness in raising the profile of the city. Located in Jiading district, the F1 site was built at a cost of USD450 million, and has a capacity of 200,000. Originally swampland, it was constructed by Shanghai Juss Corporation, Shanghai National Property Management Company Limited, and Shanghai Jia'an Investment Development Corporation. The racetrack itself took 18 months to construct from 2003, and involved over 3000 engineers. In the inaugural year 2004, the Chinese Grand Prix attracted over a quarter of a million spectators. Numbers have declined in recent years, though the extension of the franchise to 2018, the reduction in ticket prices, and the construction of a subway line to the track in 2011 were all introduced to try to address this. Shanghai's commitment to Grand Prix however is not in doubt, with Wen Zhao, deputy mayor of Shanghai, in a report for Reuters in February 2011 saying that the event is a calling card for the city and for this reason will continue to get support.

A further international event is the Shanghai Rolex Masters Tennis Tournament, held at the Qizhong Tennis Centre in Minhang District from 2009. One of the world's biggest tennis tournaments, and the only one to be staged outside North America and Europe, it is one of nine Association of Tennis Professionals Masters 1000 tournaments in the world, with prize money of over USD 3.2 million in 2012.

The Expo, International Events and the Meaning of the Shanghai's Internationalisation

One of the great issues for Shanghai is how it creates an authentic link between its history and world from which it has come, and the modernism of the present. According to local historian Peter

Hibbard, who has lived in Shanghai for over a decade and written numerous books on the development of the municipal area, one can find a strong connection between these two by seeing the city's modern vision as inspired by its wish to return to its historic status. This is a place with a powerful memory of a former period of global reach in an early phase of industrialization and the onset of modernity into China. But this memory is not a straightforward one. In a book on the 1919-1954 era in Shanghai, American academic based in the city Andrew Field writes that:

> 'The Western world often calls the years following the end of World War One in 1918 and the onset of the Great Depression in 1929 the Jazz Age. For America, an era of hedonism and wild abandon as the country celebrated the end of the Great War and the emerging global dominance of its power, industry and culture characterized in Hollywood Films from the era. For China, on the other hand, the Jazz Age signaled a period of war, calamity and violent revolution, as the young Republic struggled with the burdens of domestic warlordism and foreign imperialism.' [12]

For Field, this era was best typified by the night clubs and cabarets in Shanghai, where different segments of local and international society met each other, typifying the cosmopolitan atmosphere in this confusing, heady, sometimes reckless time. 'Within this uncertain context' Field continues, referring to the political and social chaos that sometimes reigned in the 1930s, 'China's own jazz age dawned. ...The jazz cabarets in the city during the 1920s served to blur boundaries and break barriers that separated people in their daily struggles and thus help to foster the emergence of a more cosmopolitan culture for the greater metropolis of Shanghai that would reach its flowering in the 1930s.' [13]

---

12. Andrew David Field. *Shanghai's Dancing World: Cabaret, Culture and Urban Politics 1919-1954*. The Chinese University Press, Hong Kong. 2010. p.19.
13. Ibid., p.20.

The historic imprint of this period is retained both in the cultural products from that time and their continuing resonance, but also the built environment. Writing about a new novel by local author Xiaobai, the China Daily in 2011 reported the author as saying 'Ever since Shanghai became an open harbor in the 1840s, there existed in the city a different lifestyle in the dark, completely different from that of regular citizens' daily lives. You could describe it as heart throbbing or legendary.' The report continues, 'Shanghai in the 1930s has been a favourite setting for movies and novels at home and abroad.' [14] One of the earliest of these foreign testaments to what Xiaobai rightly calls the 'legendary' nature of the city is 'Shanghai Express', which starred Marlene Dietrich and appeared in 1932. The memory of this era is also preserved in the films which China itself produced, some of the most celebrated of which starred the actress Ruan Lingyu, who was to tragically commit suicide in 1935. This period haunts not only the great buildings which line Bund, but also those which also exist throughout the concessions into which Shanghai used to be divided.

There is a great historic ambiguity over this time, however, as Field underlines. Globalization's final point, for this early phase, was to be victimization at the hands of imperialists, fragmentation of the country, and devastating war, both international and domestic. That there is not a happy memory about where the previous era of global aspirations ended means that the new phase of modernization has to be different. The Expo can be representative of this aspiration to a new type of dialogue – something which combines opening up to the world, engagement, but which also addresses what are seen as China, and the city's, specific challenges. These can be grouped broadly into challenges of society and governance, or the economy, or culture and of the environment, and it is now at these specific themes, all of them addressed during the Expo, that I will now turn.

---

14. Kun Zhang. 'Immersed once more in 1930s Shanghai'. *China Daily*, 11 February 2011

Chapter Four

Shanghai Society and Governance

How is a city growing at half a million new people a year, which plans to double its GDP in the next decade, function? How is stability achieved amongst the various complex business, government and civil groups in this city? To those visiting for the first time, Shanghai to them is the central district around the Huangpu River. But to make this city function properly, so that everything runs smoothly, and people get to work, or are able to carry out their business or their education, or get treatment at hospital, is a mammoth task. And with rising expectations towards life and public service from a rising population in the coming decade, this task is unlikely to get any easier. This chapter will describe the structures of administration that exist in Shanghai, and how they are likely to adapt and reform in the coming decade as it becomes the archetypical 'middle class' city within China in the 21st century.

These are not academic questions. Any experience of taking officials or leaders from western cities to Shanghai shows the stark difference between the demands of running a local government in a developed country, and that of trying to run an administration as vast as Shanghai now is. For the City of Liverpool, who I advised for nearly five years on their relationship with Shanghai with which they were twinned, the problem was having their leaders try to imagine being in charge of a city not of half a million as Liverpool is, but of 46 times this, and rising by the whole population of their own city each year. Seen in this light, the stable governance of Shanghai, and the vast and dramatic changes happening in the city's economy and development, are formidable and sometimes overwhelming to contemplate even for a very experienced western leader.

The aspiration to create a cohesive, sustainable city is also linked to the language used by national leaders from 2012 about a 'China Dream'. At the heart of this is the drive to have a lifestyle which is prosperous, secure and civilized for Chinese people. 'Spiritual civilization' and 'harmonious society' are also connected to these concepts. For Shanghainese, the journey to 2020 has to deliver the social infrastructure, public goods and natural environment in which they can realize this 'dream'. Like the American dream, to which it has been compared, the 'China Dream' should be available to every citizen in the city, either those long established there or those newly arrived. It has to be based on respect for fellow citizens, and for the world in which Shanghainese live. The key elements of this are for people to have the space in society to develop themselves to their full potential. As this chapter will show, education is critical to this, as is having the opportunity to realize economic and cultural potential. Shanghai is a diverse community, and one developing rapidly, The necessity to ensure that there is a framework for living in which everyone can work alongside and partnership with each other is critically important to realize this dream. Governance, welfare and social cohesion are all elements of this. These are the things this chapter will analyze.

dministrative Structures

So, in 2013, how is Shanghai governed? The city currently exists as one of the four municipalities directly under the central government in the People's Republic of China, the other three being Tianjin, Beijing and Chongqing. As such it ranks as a province level entity and gives it high status. The structure of the municipal government is given below. This shows that even in one city there is an immense range of different government organs.

Table: Shanghai Governance Structure

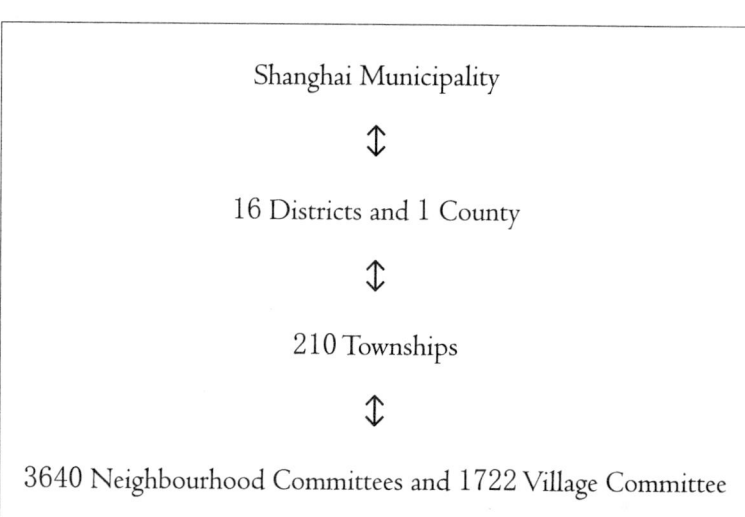

According to the 2010 census, the districts divided as follows:

District	Population (thousand)	Area (km squared)
Puxi		
Huangpu	678	20.46
Xuhui	1085	53.76
Changning	690	38.30
Jing'an	246	7.62
Putuo	1288	54.83
Zhabei	830	29.26
Hongkou	852	23.48

Yangpu	1313	60.73
Inner Suburbs		
Pudong New Area	5044	1210.41
Minhang	2429	370.75
Baoshan	1904	270.99
Jiading	1471	464.20
Outer Suburbs		
Jinshan	732	586.05
Songjiang	1582	605.64
Qingpu	1081	670.14
Fengxian	1083	687.39
County		
Chongming	703	1185.49

In 2012, Shanghai Municipality was organized with one Mayor, and eight vice mayors. This leadership group deal with issues ranging from security, budgets and implementation of the city's five year programmes. In many ways, it has a governance structure that shadows the national one of a state council which then had ministerial portfolios dealing with issues like transport, environment, industrial policy and social management.[1] Another layer of complexity is added by the fact that for each of the 16 districts, there are similar parallel structures. Pudong New Area Government, for instance, has a mayor and seven deputy mayors, who are in charge of a list of offices which includes the General Office, and then the Economy and Informationalisation Office, a Commission of Commerce, an Education Commission, a Bureau of Civil Affairs, etc.[2]

In addition to these executive administrative divisions, there is also the Shanghai Municipal Committee of the Communist Party of

---

1. Website of the Shanghai Municipal Government, www.shanghai.gov.cn
2. Website of Pudong New Area, www.pudong.gov.cn

China, which is in charge of political affairs, and the Shanghai People's Congress, and the Shanghai Chinese People's Political Consultative Conference (CPPCC).

The function of the Shanghai Municipal People's Congress is to act as a provincial equivalent of the National People's Congress, sometimes called China's parliament, which, according to the 1982 State Constitution, is the highest organ of state power within China. The Congress in Shanghai states that its main objectives are to ensure the observance and execution of the Constitution and laws, and 'to formulate and promulgate local laws and regulations under the preconditions of not contravening the Constitution.' It also has a consultative function, reviewing and approving national economic and social development plans, budgets and reports. Like the National People's Congress, the Shanghai Congress meets annually. It has a standing committee which has day to day responsibilities under a Chairman for the running of the Congress affairs, and which has Committees dealing with Law, Internal and Judicial Affairs, Finance and Economics, Education and Science and Culture, Urban Construction and Environmental Protection, Overseas, Ethnic and Religious Affairs, Foreign Affairs and Agricultural Affairs. It also has a budget, personnel, and legislative affairs commission, and a General and Research Office.[3] The current Congress has 860 members. It is reflected in congresses that reach down to township level and fulfill similar functions. Members come from varied backgrounds and are meant to represent a cross section of society.

The CPPCC Shanghai Committee is a consultative body, which convenes annually in order to give feedback and advice on draft laws, and regulations, and to discuss urban development issues. The CPPCC has 834 members, the most famous of which is probably former National Basketball Association star Yao Ming. Its membership is drawn from fields across society, including business people, cultural figures, academics and representatives from civil

---

3. Website of the Shanghai Municipal People's Congress, www.spcsc.sc.cn

society. In that sense, it has its historic roots in the national United Front established in the 1940s when the People's Republic of China was being established, and the eight patriotic parties which were recognized from that time. The advice that the CPPCC locally and nationally gives is non-binding.

Shanghai People: Yao Ming

Asked to name a current Chinese figure, most at least in the US would probably go for the baskekball star, Yao Ming. His face is certainly one of the most recognized across the world, from adverts to new reports and television. For many coming into Shanghai, he looks out from advertising boardings, and must rank as one of the great modern ambassadors for this home city. Born in Shanghai in 1980, Yao Ming has become one of China's global stars. The son of parents from the city who were 2 metres and 1.9 metres respectively, he weighed twice as much as the average Chinese when born. His career started at 13 when he practiced for ten hours a day. Entering the NBA draft in 2002, he managed to score his first basket against the Denver Nuggets the same year. Standing at 2.29 metres when fully mature, he started playing for the Shanghai Sharks for five years, before going international by moving to the American Houston Rockets in 2002. During his career, he played in the Olympics three times, in 2000, 2004 and 2008, and also in the Asian Championships and the 2006 World Championships.

While in Shanghai in 2011, Yao announced his retirement. In the final few years of his professional career, he had suffered from a number of ankle and foot injuries which had kept him out of the game. Yao is famous as a Chinese who has succeeded at one of the most competitive sports in the US, but also as the face of a number of brands, from Nike to Reebok, to Visa, McDonalds and Apple, with whom he has signed sponsorship deals. He has also supported charity events, particular during the tragic Sichuan earthquake in 2008 where he gave generously to the relief work. According to NBA Commissioner David Stern, 'Yao Ming has been a transformational player and a testament to globalization of our game. His dominant play and endearing demeanor along with his extensive humanitarian efforts have made him an international fan favourite and provided an extraordinary bridge between basketball fans in the United States and China.' [4]

A Migrant City?

Who is this administrative structure governing? Since reform and opening up began, Shanghai has undergone not just an economic transformation, but also a social one. In 1978, there were 2.9 million households, with an average of 3.8 people per house, and a population of 11 million in the whole city area. For each square kilometer of the city, there were 1785 people, with 5.42 million male and 5.55 million female. In that year, 4.5 million people worked in agriculture, and 6.45 million in non agriculture, a proportion of 58.7 per cent non agriculture based. The life expectancy was 73 years, with men living on average 70 years and women 74.

In 2011, many of these figures (with the obvious exception of life expectancy) had doubled. There were 5.2 million households, with an average number of 2.7 in each. The yearend resident population was 23 million, and the average density of people per square

---

4. Dennis Passa. 'Chinese great Yao Ming retires from basketball'. Associated Press, 20 July 2011

kilometer 3702. Of the registered population of 14 million (those who were permanent holders of Shanghai Household registration documents), this split almost 50 per cent into men and women (the women continued to slightly outnumber the men). By 2011, only 11 per cent of the city work force was in agriculture, coming in a 1.5 million. The life expectancy was 82 years, with 80 for men and 84 for women, an increase of ten years over the figure of three decades before.

The periods of most inward migration into the city were from 2000 to 2011. The growth rates are shown below. In this decade, after the entry of the country as whole to the World Trade Organisation (WTO), the city saw major inflows of people.

Table. Inward Migration Flows to Shanghai: 2000-2011

Year	Inflows Rate	Outflows Rate	Overall Increase in Population
2000	11.51	4.04	7.47
2001	11.05	4.20	6.85
2002	11.58	3.29	8.29
2003	11.15	2.76	8.39
2004	10.34	2.03	8.31
2005	9.55	2.55	7.00
2006	9.43	2.57	6.86
2007	10.70	2.88	7.82
2008	12.48	3.10	9.38
2009	11.26	3.42	7.84
2010	12.24	3.53	8.71
2011	9.29	3.76	5.53

Source: *Shanghai Statistics Yearbook 2012*, p.27

In 2011, the age structure of the city amongst the registered population was that 1.4 million were under 17 years, 3.3 million were from 18 to 34 years of age, 5.9 million were from 35 to 59 years of age, and 3.4 million were over 60. This demographic pattern of an increase in those retired over those coming into the work force was typical of developed economies from the US, to the European Union to Japan, and will be discussed later. There were also other profound social changes. Over the period from 1990 to 2011, while the number of marriages increased, the number of those which were second or third marriages doubled, and the divorce rate tripled. In 1990, there were 30 thousand divorces. By 2011, this had become 90 thousand.

What were people working in by 2011? By far the largest, over three million, were still in manufacturing. The second largest group of nearly 2 million were in retail and wholesale, with a million in construction, and 400,000 in farming. Only 200,000 were in public administration, and less than half a million in hospitality. Of the nearly 9 million people from the registered population employed in the city, 1.5 million worked for state owned enterprises, and 5 million worked in non state companies, most of these in construction or retail. There was another story that these figures showed. Between 2000 and 2011, the number of retired rose from 2.34 million to 3.63 million. In 1982, the city had 20 people who were aged over a hundred in the national census taken that year living in Shanghai area. In 2010, this had increased to 931. To put this in perspective, in the first such census carried out after the establishment of the People's Republic in 1949, that of 1953, there was only a single centurion.[5]

Compared to the Shanghai of 1978, therefore, the population of Shanghai was larger, lived longer, worked less in agriculture, had less numbers per household but also occupied less space, was more likely to work for a non state company or a foreign invested entity than a state owned one, and was more likely to have been born outside the city area and moved in. In this city, the number of those working for government running the place came in at less than 2 percent of the whole population. Shanghai in 2011 was a place with a growing population, but also an ageing population.

---

5. Zhixiong Wang; Junxian Ma. *Shanghai Statistical Yearbook*. China Statistics Press, Beijing, 2012.

The Core Issue: Inequality

Shanghai is a city with one of the highest per capita GDP's in China. But it is also a city with the same issues of inequality between the rich and the poor, with all projections showing that is likely to be maintained, or continue, into the next decade. According to the Hurun rich list on Shanghai for 2012, the city is home to 90 dollar billionaires. In 2012, 250 of them had assets of more than RMB 2 billion(USD 320 million). The top sectors for the source of these individuals wealth are property, manufacturing and investment. The youngest self made RMB billionaire is Yao Ming. 370 thousand people have RMB 6 million (USD 950 thousand) in the city, or 1 in 65 in the whole population, and 140 thousand have assets of over RMB 10 million (USD 1.6 million). This accounts for 13 per cent of the high net worth individuals in the whole country. There are 8200 super rich individuals, worth more than RMB100 million (USD 16 million), which accounts for 12 per cent of the amount for the whole of the country.[6] But there are also issues of poverty. Migrant labourers coming into the city to find work are often on low wages, many working in highly insecure seasonal employment. This issue of residence status will be looked at in more detail later. The different status of those with urban and rural household residence documents has been a heavily discussed one at national and local level for a number of years. As China has become an increasingly mobile society, with more and more people living away from their place of birth, the issue of what to do about their rights to accessing healthcare, or education in the places where they live has become a more critical one. In a moving description of migrant labourers in Xi'an by journalist Michelle Dammon Loyalka, 'Eating Bitterness', she shows the remarkable resilience, patience and stoicism of migrant labourers. They are a group which have made a major contribution to the development of modern China's economy, but also one which

---

6. www.hurun.net/userr/NewsShow.aspx?nid=217

continue to endure hardship and sacrifice. In Shanghai, as in many modern economies, the challenge of filling service jobs with far lower wages than the average has been met by the pool of migrant labourers coming into the city. But many of these are now long established, and therefore their need for access to social welfare, and in particular the rights to move their families into the urban area and allow their children to go to high school is becoming more critical. [7]

Governing Shanghai at the Grassroots

The 'Outline for the Eleventh Five Year Plan for National Economic and Social Development' issued by the City in 2006, and available on its website, sets out the key planning goals for the coming five years. Amongst its economic goals are those of resource efficiency, environmental action, and innovation, and tackling inequality. There are also sections on 'building a service orientated, accountable and law based government.'

The details of this policy are set out in the first chapter which addresses the issue the reform and opening up. In the section on social affairs, the authors state that the key objective is working 'together with the non-governmental sector in providing public goods and services.' 'The management system for public services and government procurement of services will be improved, and the non-governmental sector will be encouraged to provide public services in various ways such as supplementary investment, cooperation operation and joint equity.' The plan also asks that social institutions be cultivated and developed. 'More efforts will be made to foster non-government organizations that may implement social affairs

---

7. Michelle Dammon Loyalka. *Eating Bitterness: Stories from the Front Lines of China's Great Urban Migration*, University of California Press, Berkeley, 2012.

administration and provide public welfare services, mediate civil disputes and undertake charity work.'

The 2006 plan prefigures the language in the 2011 national Five Year Programme when it talks of social management. This context for the city is one where a huge number of newly arrived migrants mentioned above have to be absorbed not only into the local economy, but also into the society. The issue of how to do this is a pressing one. Social cohesion therefore lies at the heart of how to address social management and the provision of forms of welfare. And at the heart of this, lies the nature of citizenship and residency, and the issue of grassroots organization. 'The City,' the plan states, 'will improve grassroots democracy, seek for a democratic model and community interest coordination mechanisms that involve community inhabitants' along with representatives from the Communist Party and the government. In trying to achieve this, the plan sets a target of expanding direct elections for neighbourhood committees, with 85 per cent due to be elected by 2010.

Liu Chunrong, a researcher based at Fudan University in Shanghai, has undertaken extensive work on the building up of local forms of public participation in decision making through the creation of neighbourhood residential committees. Stating that 'the political order in Shanghai... has been established with two principles: the first is functional in the form of a danwei system based on employment; the second is a geographical one based on the place of residence,' he talks of the divisions of this latter category into municipalities, districts, resident committees, and resident's small groups.[8] From the mid-1990s, Liu states, 'the Shanghai government is interested to build up the Residence Committee institutions and to explore an alternative mode of neighbourhood governance to showcase democracy and citizenship.' He states the example of the Yinhang community, in Yangpu District, which had 120 full time professionals and neighbor representatives in 1996, and which

---

8. Chunrong Liu. 'State and Social Capital Accumulation: The Politics of Neighbourhood Council System in Shanghai'. *China Public Affairs Quarterly*, Volume 2:3, 2009, p.234.

created a structure of elected representatives to serve in committees examining citizens needs. The elections served to 'balance the dual functions of the residence committees' service to both the state and residents.'[9] In Pudong Resident Committee election laws passed in 2000 the committees had responsibilities in the areas of publicizing the constitutions and laws, upholding rights of residents, protecting public property, mediating in civil disputes, managing public affairs, maintaining social order evaluating social workers performances, mobilizing the community to serve residents, and canvassing local opinion to feed upwards to the municipal government.[10] Within this experimentation, 'the scheme of urban community building which involves a variety of processes such as Party cell networking and election mobilization have created a particular political opportunity structure for the engagement of residents in the neighbourbood problem solving.' In particular, these residence committees, with an infrastructure of direct elections, could help a society going through such rapid and sometimes disorientating change, to 'negotiate a meaning of community.'[11]

The lived experience of many arriving in the city, whatever their profession and wherever they have come from, is an important consideration. Issues of social cohesion refer to the ways in which different groups, with their diverse view points, their expectations and their demands on the social infrastructure of a society, are able to get along together without explosions of anger or frustration. Alienation can occur when a city grows as quickly as Shanghai, and the citizens have little sense of belonging to the place, or any sense of invested social capital there. Even on current projections, Shanghai's population will increase by half a million people each year, rising to 28 million by 2020. According to one researcher based at the Shanghai Academy of Social Sciences (SASS), the most extreme estimate is that each person can have 100 square metres of

---

9. Ibid., p.243.
10. Ibid., p.244.
11. Ibid., p.261.

built space. In that sense, the city can expand further and still be able to accommodate many more people. if land is used efficiently and productively. Parts of Shanghai are semi urban, rather than fully built up, and in these areas the density of people per square kilometer is much lower. The term coined for this at SASS is 'the new rural'. Industrial zones in the city in particular, which are no longer used as manufacturing is moved out to neighbouring provinces or deeper into China can be converted to residential use (this will be covered in the chapter on the environment). The zoning patterns in the past too are now superseded by mixed use of land. In this sense, according to the researcher, Hong Kong is a good example to look at, with its economically multi-functional communities.

But this is the hard infrastructure of society. What about the software? Residence rights mentioned above are intimately linked to this issue of community building and the software for that. Rural household registrations documents holders limitations to the claims they can make off social welfare, despite the fact that many are long term citizens of the city, making tax payments there and having property and interests seems to fly in the face of intuitions about social justice. Many from the neighbouring province of Zhejiang who have succeeded in business, for instance, have apartments in the city, but limits to the ways in which they can use hospitals or the education system. One unexpected issue is that the city's need to attract well qualified people from other areas of the country will mean a good population supply – taking in people of working age. Half a million people a year coming in therefore is not a burden, but a necessity, brought about by the dynamism of the city and its economic needs. Enfranchising these newly arrived people and making them feel properly 'Shanghainese' is a major challenge.

The sense of 'Shanghai' identity deserves deeper thought. What are the core values and identifications for a resident in Shanghai in the 21st century? How does one regulate the relationship between old and new Shanghainese? This is not just about external city branding, but about how residents, through their diverse experiences of the city, internalize the identity of the place within themselves. In what ways do they feel like they 'belong' to the city, and have vested interests in its success? Are they able to feel that they are 'as Shanghainese' as those who were born and brought up in the place? In this area, the floating population who constitute over a third of the city's current residents, are critical. Their sense of belonging, despite their being from other places, often speaking in other dialects, and having different memories and expressions of identity than those who were born in Shanghai, is a major issue. The city's culture has to accommodate and embrace diverse groups, especially as they contribute to the economic growth and the tax revenues of the municipality. At the heart of this lies the issue of education.

Shanghai People: Liu Xiang

Liu Xiang was born in July 1983 in Putuo District, Shanghai, and is one of the great 110 metre hurdlers of modern times. He is the first ever Chinese winner of an Olympic track and field gold medal. While Chinese athletes have excelled increasingly in the last few years in swimming, athletics and wrestling, track and field has been one area where they have had the greatest challenges to succeed. Liu Xiang's achievement in simultaneously holding the world record, the world championship and the Olympics gold medal was a first.

Liu made his debut in the Asian games in Japan in 2001. His record beating performance in the 2004 Olympics in Athens was a seminal moment. In both the Beijing 2008 and the London 2012 Olympics, however, he was less successful, having to withdraw from both because of injury. Team leader Feng Shuyong stated after his final withdrawal, 'What Liu Xiang did today reflected the true Olympic spirit. Winning is not so important, participation is what matters. We have all seen how hard it is for him. It is such a pity but his spirit is there.' British hurdler

Andy Turner commented, 'I regard him as probably the best hurdler in history and have so much respect for him. It was horrible seeing him limp off like that.' But Liu's legacy is secure. Usain Bolt, the Jamaican world record holding sprinter and gold medalist stated that Liu was a great athlete. One of the most amazing things is that he came back. He switched legs and started leading with a different leg. He's a true champion.' [12]

Education

Most people when asked, would state that education is critical to the future of a country or a society, and that investments in education and in human capital will only grow more important in the era of late modernity. In the high tech industries and in the service sectors in which most jobs are expected to be created in the future, the supply of well educated people in sciences, languages, and humanities will be increasingly important. As industrialization spreads throughout the world, the manufacturing and export based growth model on which China has built much of its success since the late 1970s will be replaced by a journey up the value added tree, and the need for indigenously trained inventors, creators and company personnel.

Shanghai's provision of education to primary and university students will be critical. In 1978, Shanghai had 50 thousand people in institutions of higher education, and 1 million in secondary schools, and 870 thousand in primary schools. By 2011, the numbers going to university had risen to 500 thousand, with 730 thousand in secondary schools and 730 thousand too in primary schools. This shows that the numbers of those going on to tertiary level education

---

12. 'Liu Xiang Crashes Out Olympics but Wins Respect'. Xinhua News Agency, 8 August 2012.

has increased tenfold, even though, through ageing population, the numbers at secondary and primary school have actually decreased. From a smaller student base, more are going on to get degrees. From 2000 through to 2011, 99.9 per cent of children of the appropriate age went to primary school, with 97 per cent going on to secondary school. From 2000 to 2011, the rate of those going on to university rose from 67 per cent to 87 per cent. Across the city, in 2011, there were 754 secondary schools, with 51 thousand teachers and 591 thousand enrolments. There were 764 primary schools, with 46 thousand full time teachers, and 731 thousand student enrolments.[13] In Shanghai, education is big business and something that families make major investments in.

In the critical area of universities, from 2000 to 2011 the number of those defined as 'regular institutions of higher education' rose from 37 to 66, with a rise in staff from 60 thousand to 70 thousand. Of these, the number of academic staff rose from 30 thousand to nearly 40 thousand. In 2000, 40 thousand graduated from universities, but by 2011 this had risen to 130 thousand. Student enrollment across all the institutions for higher education rose from 220 thousand to 510 thousand. This despite the fact that in all other areas, the numbers of students and teachers and institutions at primary and secondary level fell, simply because of the demographics of the city and the fact that the population was rising because people were moving in after they had completed their education elsewhere.

For these 40 thousand teachers at institutions of higher education in 2011, the most were teaching engineering (over a quarter of the overall amount, at 11,343) and literature (8746). There were 4003 teaching science, 3496 teaching education, 2567 teaching economics, 2494 teaching law, and 2864 teaching administration, with 2348 teaching medicine. Of the 66 institutes of higher education across the city, a mere three were comprehensive universities, with 25 specialising in science and technology, 18 in economics and finance,

---

13. Zhixiong Wang; Junxian Ma. op. cit., pp.374-390.

five art schools, 3 politics and law schools, and 3 medical schools. Of the 84 thousand that graduated from these universities and institutes 27 thousand were in engineering, 14 thousand in literature, 17 thousand in administration, 8 thousand in economics, 5 thousand in law, and 6 thousand in science.

One can therefore say that in the period 2000 to 2011, the city's various districts had changed the configuration of their education system, to become focused on tertiary education. And the main students they produced were in engineering, and sciences, but also in literature.

There is an intimate link between education and globalization. In raw numbers, Shanghai had 18,351 international students in 2011, up from 13,691 in 2005. But the vast majority of these were from Asia – over 12,182 in 2011. Europeans made up 3257, Africans 1233, and North Americans 1239. In terms of quality of education, again, Shanghai's universities do not yet appeal in global ranking tables. The Times Higher Education World University Rankings for 2012 to 2013, powered by Thomson Reuters and released on 17th December placed Fudan University at 207th, and Shanghai Jiaotong University at 294th.[14] In the Quality and Success rankings, Fudan came in in 2012 at 90th, Shanghai Jiaotong at 125th, and Tongji University at 451.

According to an assessment for the Organisation for Economic Cooperation and Development (OECD) in 2010, Shanghai's educational system was seen as 'very effective.' It was found that students were 'exposed to a much broader knowledge base and are trained to integrate their knowledge and tackle real life problems.' The report continues, 'All these changes are markedly different from the traditional Chinese pattern in which students learn subjects by heart and regurgitate such knowledge in examinations.' However, the report concludes:

---

14. www.timeshighereducation.co.uk/work-university-rankings/2012-13

'... the changes in student learning were brought about chiefly by organized and structured top-down reforms, implemented either through examinations or policy shifts. Such measures may be well designed, but students are still not given much autonomy in their study. Schools with outstanding characteristics are still rare and examination pressure still prevails.'

Students are seen as having little time and space for learning on their own. 'There is an opportunity cost in terms of time and space', an observer noted. 'Students grow within narrow margins and are not fully prepared for their lives and work in the future. This is seen as a deep crisis, exacerbated by the reality of single-child families.' [15]

One area of real development will be international co-operation in education, something that has been pioneered over the last decade with the establishment of a full campus in partnership with Nottingham University from the UK at Ningbo in Zhejiang province, and a cooperation with Shanghai Jiaotong University and Liverpool University in Suzhou. For Shanghai, the biggest development in this sector in the last few years has been the establishment of a campus from New York University in the Pudong area, which was approved by the central Chinese Minister of Education in 2012, and as of 2013 is now being constructed, with inaugural classes starting in August. 300 student places are planned, with over half local Chinese, and the rest from outside China. Shanghai is New York University's second international degree-granting campus, with Abu Dhabi predating it. On its website, the campus describes itself as 'making the world your major' and goes on to map out its vision:

'NYU Shanghai exemplifies the highest ideals of contemporary higher education by uniting the intellectual resources of New York University's global network with the multi-dimensional greatness of China. It guides

---

15. 'Strong Performers and Successful Reformers in Education: Lessons from Pisa for the United States', OECD, 2010, p.98.

students towards academic and moral excellence, preparing them for leadership in all walks of life, and it contributes to the endless quest for new insights in the human condition and the natural world.' [16]

This level of co-operation is complicated. It remains a highly protected sector in most countries. The national Minister of Education have been highly cautious in authorizing such joint ventures. The simple fact is, though, that with over 1 million students from China having been abroad in the last two decades to study, and with the demand for education rising, there is now critical need for more diversity in the internal system to satisfy some of this demand. In that sense, NYU Shanghai is an incubator for possibilities into the future of how foreign universities might educate Chinese in partnership locally without needing the students to leave China. It also goes some way towards meeting the likely future demand for non Chinese students who wish to study in China.

Healthcare

Healthcare is one of the key development issues for any city in China in the coming decade, just as it is in Europe or North America. Healthcare has been a particular focus of Five Year Planning at national level. As Baogang Guo commented in a study on the Chinese national healthcare system, 'cost, access and quality are three important values in healthcare…. Since 1979, China has attempted to use market mechanisms to restructure its outdated healthcare system and improve its coverage and delivery systems.' Marketisation

---

16 From the University Shanghai website, www.shanghai.nyu.edu/about/who-we-are, accessed 7 July 2013

was one of the main tools by which China tried to address the shortcomings of a system in a country in which people were living longer and expecting much more from their care. With the slow disappearance of the work unit supplied healthcare insurance, more people in work have taken out insurance, although the results of this have been very uneven. Mandatory urban residence insurance was created in 2010, a system which also extended to migrant labourers. Debates about further healthcare reform divide between those who want more marketisation, and those who demand an active role for the state because of the social importance of good health and wellbeing.

As Guo notes, 'one of the major problems with China's existing health care system is that health care resources are not distributed equitably.' City residents in any case get a good deal, but even within municipalities like Shanghai there are differences between what access different social groups get to healthcare, and how good the quality is. The State Council has since 2006 set out discussions on a new comprehensive health care reform proposal, with 2020 as the date for the final establishment of a new system. For this system, the government still has an important role, providing critical budgetary support. As part of the fiscal stimulus package brought in after the economic crisis in 2008, funding was provided by the government to expand health care to 90 per cent of the population, and to create a national list of prescribed drugs from which patients can chose, as well as improving the health care delivery system. A major issue is to 'promote equality in basic health services' and eliminate surcharges on drugs.'

The healthcare sector in Shanghai has seen major rationalization since 1978. In that year, there were 388 hospitals, and 4823 health care institutions. These have now fallen to 308 and 3358 respectively. Instead, there are now many more doctors per 10 thousand people – 5.21 in 2011 compared to 3.35 in 1978. And a similar rise in the number of medical professionals – 13.91 per 10 thousand people in 2011 compared to 8.5 thirty years previously. Causes of death in

Shanghai in 2011, similar to other developed regions, were mainly circulation diseases (35 per cent of mortalities in that year), tumours (31 per cent), respiratory problems (10 per cent), metabolic diseases (4 per cent) and then a mixture of digestive, infectious, nervous and genitourinary diseases. [17] Surprisingly, the death rate of infants rose from 2009 to 2011, changing from 2.89 per thousand to 5.70 per thousand, and the death rate of pregnant women or women giving birth from 7 per hundred thousand in 2009 to 7.36 per hundred thousand in 2011.

One of the greatest healthcare issues highlighted from the mortality figures given above is the rise in heart disease because of obesity. The rapid change of diet in the city through the increase in meat consumption, the rise of fast food shops and the increase in convenience food has taken its toll, along with the changes in lifestyles. People eat more saturated fats, but they also live more sedentary lives. According to analysts Paul French and Matthew Crabbe, 'By 2008 – China's Olympic year – the number of obese and overweight people in the country topped more than a fifth of China's adult population.' [18] Looking to 2015, the authors predict that as many as 200 million Chinese will be morbidly obese within five years. 'China is on course to be exactly like the US in approximately 10 to 20 years.' [19] Obesity has brought about a rise in the rates of diabetes, and hepatitis. In particular, obesity has increased in Children affecting as many as one in five in Shanghai. [20] Increase of salt intake because of its high presence in processed foods has also caused health problems, linked to heart and circulation diseases. Quoting the British Medical Journal in March 2005, French and Crabbe spell out the costs for the healthcare system if obesity is not addressed:

'China has 160 million people with hypertension and

---

17. Zhixiong Wang; Junxian Ma. op. cit., p.397
18. Paul French; Matthew Crabbe. *Fat China : How Expanding Waistlines Are Changing a Nation*. Anthem Press, London, 2010, p.13.
19. Ibid., p.15.
20. Ibid., p.10.

another 160 million with hyperlipidaemia. Assuming the daily cost to be RMB 1 for antihypertensive drugs and RMB 2 for cholesterol lowering drugs, a conservative estimate for the total drug cost would be RMB 175 billion a year if these patients were given drug treatment. This alone would consume almost a third of the total healthcare expenditure of the country.' [21]

As French and Crabbe state, 'It is not clinics and hospitals that create improvements in people's eating and living habits and ultimately improve people's understanding of the obesity issues; it is the healthcare professionals within those institutions who impart their advice and knowledge that are the key to changing the increasingly entrenched eating habits that have emerged to create obesity problems.' [22]

Ranged alongside obesity as an avoidable burden on the healthcare system are issues around smoking and, to a less extent, alcoholic consumption, both of which have risen in the last decade – with smoking now becoming more popular amongst younger men and women in urban areas like Shanghai. Adopting the same fierce legislation against tobacco advertising is one way of trying to manage this impending crisis.

What is less avoidable is the simple fact that Shanghai is now an ageing city, and one with a large increase of those living to be over 80. The mixture of this with the fact that most households now are highly mobile, with many living apart from their parents, and the fact that the impact of the one child policies in the 1970s onwards means there are far fewer young to look after elderly parents means that there is a demographic time bomb. In terms of pension payments and the increase of possible healthcare costs and care costs, the next decade will almost certainly see a major challenge to China's social welfare system. Shanghai will also be part of this, with immense

---

21. Ibid., pp.200–201.
22. Ibid., p.201.

burdens on its social welfare infrastructure. Policy responses are happening now but they will need continuing major commitment to be successful.

Social Welfare

In 2000, Shanghai had 2 million retired staff, either from government units or workers with medicare. In 2011 this had risen to 4.04 million. In that period, the minimum pension per month has increased from RMB 445 to 1280. From 2005 to 2011 the number of nursing homes for the elderly grew from 13 to 15, however the number of people spending time in these institutions has grown from 4300 to 11,400. The costs for families and for the state for funding the retirement of people as they live longer are growing. We can give a tangible measure to how much more important this is becoming: 'It may come as a surprise to many readers that the most expensive function of the Chinese government (including central and local levels) is not urban construction, infrastructure, or even national defense but, instead, the provision of public pensions,' as Mark Frazier, an American Academic, has written.

That society is developing dramatically because of the fundamental change in the economy is obvious. What is less easy to understand is the ways in which this impacts on the welfare of individuals. In November 2012, a case similar to those that have occurred in Japan and Europe in developed societies happened – with the discovery of a man's body several months after he had died. 51 year old Qian Zhonghong, who was unmarried, was found dead in his kitchen after police broke into his house in Zhonglie on the 3 November. Xu Chunxian, director of the local neighbourhood committee, stated, according to the report in the local press, that while the committee 'was in frequent touch with lonely elderly people aged above 65,' they had 'never thought about middle-aged people who lived alone.'[23] Issues of those who live alone and simply fall through the social safety net because of the immense business and preoccupation of the rest of the society are only likely to increase.

Using social welfare to deal with the problems of inequality has been a central theme of the development plans over the period of the 11th and 12th Five Year Programmes. Means by which to build social capital and cohesion in a society are also uppermost in officials' and administrators' minds. Civil organizations have increased in number since 2005, with a rise of 7556 which were registered in 2005 to 10,385 in 2011, of which a third were social organizations and two thirds civil non-enterprises. There were also a small number of foundations. Philanthropy has also increased, with more of the wealthy giving to charities or foundations. In the next decade, as the numbers of newcomers into the city increases, this is only likely to rise in importance. The harmonious interaction between civil society and government has to deepen, with a more enabling legal environment and more creative acceptance of the ways in which civil society can contribute to social cohesion and stability.

The Role of International Migration and Citizens

Shanghai has always been a place where people from the international community came. In the early 20th century it was a magnet for business people from Europe and the US, living in the city,

---

23. *Shanghai Daily*, 5 November 2012

establishing businesses there. One of the most famous of these was Carl Crow, author of the celebrated book '400 Million Customers' published in 1937 and one of the earliest pieces to talk up the possibilities of the China market. Crow was to establish newspapers in Shanghai, and be active in the city for over three decades until the Japanese invasion forced him to move initially to Chongqing and then back to Manhattan, where he died in 1945 at the end of the war. Crow was one amongst a large, heterodox group of foreigners who had made Shanghai their home in the first half of the 20th century. With the opening up of China to foreign investment after 1978, more foreigners have come to live in the city, making it the most popular place for ex-pats to be based amongst major Chinese cities.

According to the 2010 national census, Shanghai has over 208 thousand expats registered as living in the city area. 143 thousand of these were from outside greater China, with 19 thousand from Hong Kong SAR, 910 from Macau SAR and 45 thousand from Taiwan. The creation of direct air links between Taipei and Shanghai has started to have an impact on the number of Taiwanese now based in Shanghai, making it much easier for them to return home to see family and do business.

Just as they did over half a century before, expats make a particular contribution to the atmosphere of the city. A book profiling various different foreigners living in Shanghai, states that of the foreigners now residing there they are 'an eclectic bunch, with businessmen, builders, thinkers, artists, and performers and a few teachers thrown in... In truth most expats defy such easy expectations.' The book describes a British academic who now works as a film maker, an Israeli working as a fashion designer, a French flower display designer, and a former American physicist who has now become a writer. Their perceptions of Shanghai differ widely. For one, 'It is a city of contrasts,' and to another it is a city where 'everything is possible.'[24]

Attracting international human capital will be a major challenge

---

24. *Expat Tales in Shanghai*, Better Link Press, Shanghai, 2011

for Shanghai, however. Its plans for development and for the internationalization of its finance sector (see later) will depend on having well qualified people, many of whom will come from abroad. Surveys in the mid 2000s showed that despite producing huge numbers of graduates, China still had a critical lack of internationally qualified senior managers. While many overseas Chinese students are now returning to China to work, they are largely inexperienced. The need for people who have over a decade of work experience in their sector is growing. And recruiting the best people from abroad to come and live in the city will be important in the coming decade. The living environment of Shanghai will be an important consideration for those who are headhunted to take up senior positions. Schools offering courses up to international standards, healthcare for expats, and the quality of the natural environment are all important. Getting good people from the finance sector to work in the city will mean attracting them not just with competitive salary packages, but also with reassurances about schools for their children, and flexible visa arrangements for their partners. The ease of doing business in the city will be critical. In the 2013 'Ease of Doing Business' survey produced each year by the International Finance Corporation, China came 91st globally out of 185 countries and territories, the same rank it had occupied the year before. Marks for starting a business, dealing with construction permits and getting electricity and paying taxes were particularly low. The strongest area was in enforcing contracts and registering property. In starting a business, China requires 13 procedures against a figure of 7 elsewhere in East Asia and 5 on average across the OECD, 33 days as compared to 12 in the OECD, and the highest levels of paid in capital. Only in terms of cost as a percentage of the income of the business did China outperform the OECD.[25] Singapore and Hong Kong SAR came first and second in the global rankings respectively. This is an indication of how much work Shanghai needs to do in order to attract international human capital. It is still a city regarded as being one that requires special skills from expats working there in

---

25. Data at www.doingbusiness.org/data/exploreeconomies/china/, accessed 12 January 2013

international sectors rather than as a place where any mainstream finance professional might consider living.

Shanghai 2020: The Creation of a Middle Class Society

If the objective of the national government is to become a middle income country within a decade, then for Shanghai where per capita GDP levels are already at the middle income level, the objective has to be to become an exemplar of a middle class city – a city with what is called a 'diamond shaped' social structure, in which there are few at the top, few at the bottom and the majority in the middle. This would be the ideal social structure.

One of the most important possibilities open for administrators in the city is that of e-governance. Information technology creates important new possibilities for citizens to engage with decision making, and to see transparency from their local and national government. China passed an Open Governance Law nationally in 2008, granting citizens the rights to request information from the government. Some have placed budgets online for scrutiny, and in other areas it has been used for scrutiny of new laws, before submission to the National People's Congress. All of these innovations have been used down to the most basic unit of governance in China. Online users now number close to a billion in China, with usage in Shanghai covering almost all groups. E-governance improvements have been a key objective of the Shanghai municipality in the last decade, and offer ways in which it can experiment in getting feedback on how it is able to deliver services and how it is performing.

Shanghai's expansion will need more migrants, and in fact an increase in the number of those coming into the city, with up to half a million a year. This is a greater figure than has ever before been accommodated. The impact of this migration on the transport system, the waste management system, the healthcare and education system and on the social welfare of the city will be huge. But like elsewhere, migrants are necessary because they address the issue of an ageing population, and also they bring an economically dynamic group of on the whole highly aspirational people who will be able to make positive contributions to the city's development.

These newcomers have to be enfranchised into the identity of the city. They need to internalize the meaning of what it is to be resident of Shanghai, and to belong to Shanghai. They need to feel that they are welcome and that they are able to find lifestyles there which suit them. The creation of hubs or clusters where people from specific regions of China some, while it is acceptable in the short term, may well lead to issues of division and social tension. Having large, very demarcated outsider communities within the city may well give rise to resentment amongst longer term inhabitants. Integration policies are important. At the heart of this is flexibility over household registration documents and the rights these give to access to local services.

The definition of 'middle class' is highly contentious in China, with much argument over what constitutes a middle class and whether this can be derived solely from their earning levels or from other measurables. But in Shanghai, as one analyst said, we see the same kind of high consuming, high earning, homeowner and well educated middle class patterns we see elsewhere in the world. These people are stakeholders in the economic success of their communities and their country because they own or have interests in property through leases, have jobs in which they have invested, or even own their own companies. In that sense, the rise in the people that fit this demographic is important, because this will create the society which Shanghai will become in the coming decade. Shanghai cannot be a city of the super rich or the mega wealthy elite. These only constitute a tiny minority of the population. It can become a city of the middle class, service orientated and well educated.

One of the great challenges of the next decade, at primary and high school level, is to change the culture of education towards more pupil centred patterns of education, in which the curricular is more geared towards individuals taking initiative and solving problems on their own. Creative education is important. This will also mean that moral education will also become more important. Shanghai does not wish to see a hedonistic, self centred generation who are interested only in furthering their own agenda and looking after their own networks. Once more, it needs to be a city of stakeholders, who feel that they belong and that they are joined to other members of their society in the success of their city. The ways in which the city creates this sort of corporate identity and sense of spiritual and not just economic belonging will be critical.

For the secondary education sector, by 2020 Shanghai must aspire to have world class universities. It has made huge investments in the tertiary educational system, and can see a big increase in the number of graduates. However, its universities are competent at the moment and not truly world class. They need to aim to be far higher in international ranking tables by 2020, taking in more international teachers, and aiming to recruit more international students, and also creating more strategic links with other major universities. They need to be more profoundly globalised that they currently are.

Shanghai is representative of the modern networked society. As early as 2001, there were five million mobile phone users in the city. By 2011, the city ranked top in the whole country for mobile phones registered, with an astonishing 121 for every 100 people.[26] Broadband speeds were also the fastest in the country. The networked society will shop, live and socialize in different ways, and the impact of this will be felt up to 2020. The impacts of networking are little understood at present, but the ways in which social capital and cohesion can be created through these new networks is already

---

26. People's Daily Online, 11 February 2011

becoming clear. Shanghai stands well placed to be one of the best networked cities by 2020, and one in which innovations in the way in which business and administration is done through these networks and the ways in which they impact on the interface between customers and citizens and service providers from the state and non state sector will be critical.

The impact of ageing and of lifestyle choices through diet, stress and other factors mean that the healthcare sector in the coming decade will be critical. There is no doubt that education needs to be developed about diet choices, and about well being beyond simply physically looking after people. Already there are signs that the same issues of alienation and depression that occur in developed societies are now also occurring in Shanghai. The liquidity of life in a city as vast and as mobile as Shanghai means that rootlessness, anxiety and stress are all due to increase. A report issued in 2008 by the Chinese Association for Mental Health stated that Chinese people between 15 and 34 were the most likely to commit suicide because of the pressures on them.[27] And while rates have subsequently seen a decline, China still has some of the highest rates for women in the world. Mental health needs investment in terms of the training of professionals and the supply of facilities to deal with this area. Wellbeing needs to be explicitly figured into urban planning, with support for research and understanding. The sheer speed of change in the city will have an impact on the ways in which people live and operate there. The need for them to be equipped to cope with these rapid changes is very high. Shanghai in 2020 needs to exemplify city living not just in the built environment, but in the rise of a new social configuration and in the creation of new modes of living between diverse groups who are able to live in a competitive and highly dynamic environment but one in which they are able to live fulfilled, happy lives. The support of civic society and of the creation of community will be critical to this. This will be a theme returned to in the chapter on culture.

---

27. Quoted by BBC, 10 September 2008

Chapter Five

The Shanghai Economy

The economy of Shanghai is one of the most dynamic growth engines of modern China. 'With only 0.06% of the nation's land area, Shanghai contributes 4.1% of China's GDP.'[1] Shanghai's ports handle 8% of the nation's total freight, and the city sees 12 per cent of the whole of China's imports and exports. In a number of other indicators, from Research and Development spending (6.6 % of China's total) to patent applications (5.4%) to foreign direct investment (10 %) and retails sales (3.7 per cent of the nations total) Shanghai punches above its weight.

It is in this zone of economic growth that many of the achievements of the last decades have happened, and they have left a visible imprint on the landscape. But it is also in the area of economics where some of the greatest future challenges lie. The city has set itself the four objectives in the next decade of becoming a regional centre for finance, services, trade, and the economy. The launch of the China (Shanghai) Pilot Free Trade Zone by the end of September 2013 will, in particular, exert huge influence upon the future of this city. This chapter will look at how the city is likely to develop over this period. But in order to do that, we have to first review where the city has come since 1978, and in particular since it became a special economic zone

---

1. Information Office of Shanghai Municipality. *Shanghai Basic Facts 2011*, Shanghai Municipal Statistics Bureau, 2011, p.15.

in 1990.

The Phases of Development

Under the successive Five Year Plans and Programmes since the 1990s, the priority of the city has been the opening up of special areas, in particular Pudong, and the internationalization of the economy. At the heart of this has been a profound engagement with marketisation. The main economic sectors in this have been construction and the transition from a manufacturing to a services led economy. The role of land has been critical, with land prices partially marketised in the last few years. Another key element is the role of capital investment, in building infrastructure and developing commercial and other construction projects.

From 1978 to 2012 the Gross Domestic product of the city increased 24 times. The main area for increase in this period has been in construction and tertiary industry. The period of most explosive growth however was from 1997, where, like the rest of the country, the entry to the World Trade Organisation in 2001 marked a new era of immense productivity. [2] We can track the rise of the importance of tertiary sector and the shift away from industry in the proportion of the GDP since 1978:

Table: Sectoral Structure of Shanghai GDP 1978-2011

Year	GDP	Primary Industry	Industry	Construction	Tertiary Industry
1978	100	4%	76%	1.3%	18%
1990	100	4%	60%	5%	31%
2000	100	1.6%	41%	4%	52%
2011	100	0.7%	37.6%	4%	58%

Source: Zhixiong Wang; Junxian Ma. *Shanghai Statistical Yearbook 2012*. China Statistics Press, Beijing, 2012, p.49.

---

2. Zhixiong Wang, Junxian Ma. op. cit., p.48.

But this is not just a story of changes in sectoral balance in the macro-economy. For human development, this three decade period has also been one of the most remarkable in terms of statistics undergone by any society in history. In 1978, the per capita GDP was RMB 2485 per annum. By 2011 this had risen to 82,560, an increase of almost 35 times. The USD rate for this is in the table below:

Table: Shanghai Per Capita GDP – RMB and USD from 1978 to 2011

Year	Per Capita GDP RMB	Per Capital GDP USD
1978	2485	1445
1990	5911	1236
2000	30047	3630
2011	82560	12784

By 2011, therefore, Shanghai's per capita GDP was the highest among all China's provinces, autonomous regions and cities directly under the central government.

The underlying tale of this transition is shown in the way in which the service sector is now the engine of Shanghai's growth. There has been an historic shift away from manufacturing and heavy industry. Retail and wholesale industries, the financial industry, real estate, leasehold and business services, transportations, warehousing and post have all seen dramatic increases in the last decades. According to an analyst for a major bank based in Shanghai speaking in late 2012, the city shows the future of consumption in China. This is clear in the steep increase in retail over 2001 to 2011. In 2001, retail and wholesale industries grew 15 per cent over the previous year. In 2011 they maintained double digit growth, with a 12.6 per cent rise, figures far ahead of any other area of China. It is clear from this that Shanghai is a consumption driven economy in ways that the rest of China is aiming towards.

Shanghai was once regarded as the home of the only authentic industrial proletariat within China in the 1920s. This was one of the reasons why the early Communist Party held its first congress in the city in 1921, in a location still preserved today near the city hall in Xintiandi. But as a result of economic development and change, the city is now home more to services, research and development, and emerging hi tech sector goods than to manufacturing, which has moved either south or inland where labour costs are lower. In fact, Shanghai has now become a consumer of the goods from other provinces.

Shanghai's Industrial Brands

Shanghai is still home to some of the key heavy industry names in China, despite the transformation of its economy to service sector and tertiary industry rather than primary or secondary industry in the last three decades. Some of the best known names are profiled here.

Baosteel Group: Headquartered in a building named after the company in Pudong, Baosteel ranks second in the world in terms of steep output, behind ArcelorMittal of India, producing 44 million tonnes annually (about 7 per cent of the country's total). Derived from changes made in 1978 when the original plant was built in Baoshan suburb, Shanghai, with Japanese investment and technology, (according to the Baosteel company website, construction started only one day after the closing of the Third Plenum of the Eleventh Communist Party Central Committee, which announced the Reform and Opening Up process, on 23rd December 1978), Baosteel was the result of mergers made in 1998 between the Baoshan Iron and Steel Corporation, the Shanghai Metallurgical Holding Group Corporation, and the Shanghai Meishan

Group Company. Listed on the Shanghai Stock Exchange, it has also considered an Initial Public Offering in Hong Kong. The company has plants throughout China, including a major new one in Guangdong Province, and has a strategic relationship with ThyssenKrupp of Germany. In September 2012 it had to suspend production at one of its plants in Shanghai due to falling domestic demand on the back of weak global economic growth.[3] As of 2012, the company employs 116 thousand people around the world, ranking 197th in the 2012 Fortune Global 500.

Shanghai's prominence as a logistics centre and as a port (see below) has already been mentioned. It is not surprising therefore that in Jiangnan Shipyard Group Corporation Ltd it has one of the world's largest civil and defense shipbuilders. Founded in 1865, during the Qing dynasty, the shipyard is now located in Changxing island, where it has a number of super dry docks. Its former location was in the city, near to the location where the Shanghai Expo was held. The company now specializes in building naval vessels, merchant ships, ocean going facilities, and has the capacity to manage large sized steel structures and pressure vessels. In particular, it produces car carriers, liquefied gas carriers, crude oil tankers, Panamax bulk carriers, and multi-purpose cargo ships. As an enterprise, it has been highly innovative, throughout the period after 1949 when it came under the State Shipbuilding Corporation. It made the first sea crossing train ferry in China, the first ocean exploration and communication ship, the first liquid petroleum tanker and the first ten thousand tonne hydraulic forging press. It employs 10,500 people, with 750 engineers and technicians, and 2700 technical personnel.

The steep increase in car usage in China in the last two decades meant that, by 2009, China overtook the USA as the main global market for cars. Car numbers in Shanghai have increased to 2 million, half the number in Beijing, but still a massive increase for a city that had very

---

3. Reuters, 27 September 2012

few cars before 1980. SAIC Motor Corporation Limited (previously known as Shanghai Automotive Industry Corporation) is headquartered in the city, and is one of the big four national automotive companies, producing in 2011 nearly 4 million vehicles, making it the largest producer in the country. Established in 1955, as Shanghai City Diesel Parts Manufacturing Company, it merged with the Shanghai City Power Equipment Manufacturing Company in 1958 to become the Shanghai City Power Manufacturing Company and produced its first car, the Phoenix, in September that year. The company changed names again in 1960, and the Phoenix was renamed the 'Shanghai Car' in 1964 with capacity reaching 5000 a decade later. In 1969, the company was called the Shanghai City Tractor and Automotive Industry Company, and was amongst the first to send out a delegation in 1982 to West Germany to view production there. A result of this was that Volkswagen allowed the company to produce Santanas in Shanghai from the following year. The VW company formally created a joint venture with the Shanghai partner in 1984, called the Shanghai Volkswagen Automobile Company. This has proved to be one of the most enduring and successful joint ventures since 1979. Shanghai Automotive Industry was set up in 1990, producing 100 000 Santana cars by 1993. In 1997, the company was listed on the Shanghai Stock Exchange, issuing 300 million A shares. By 2005, after further restructuring, the company reached its target of producing a million cars a year, and in the following year came 475th in the Fortune 500 World rankings, with sales revenue of over USD 14 billion. By 2008 this had reached USD 22 billion, making it 373rd. In 2010 it produced 3.58 million cars, and had opened facilities in the US, and the UK, at Longbridge, home of the MG Rover production line. It employs 104 000 people globally.

The transformation of Shanghai's economy can also be seen in the change from public and state owned enterprises to non-state and private. This trend has been ongoing over the last 15 years, with the formal acceptance of the role of non-state companies as engines of GDP growth at the 16th Party Congress in 2002 when the Three Represents acknowledging the role of the non state sector was written into the Party constitution. The table below shows the dramatic change in the last two decades of how much GDP is produced by state and non state companies.

Table: Division Between State, Non State and Other Ownership Structures in Shanghai, 1990-2011

Year	Composition of GDP (100)	State owned	Collective owned	Non Public owned	(Proportion of Non Public Owned of which is classified as Private)
1990	100	71.2	24.2	4.6	2.9
1995	100	59.6	22.3	18.1	7.7
2000	100	55.0	16.4	28.6	13.1
2005	100	48.4	8.5	43.1	21.00
2011	100	45.1	4.8	50.1	24

In a little over two decades, Shanghai has travelled from a city where over 95 per cent of the city's GDP was produced by state or collective owned enterprises, to one now where it balances almost exactly between non-state and state ownership. This almost exactly reflects the conclusions of the OECD report on China in September 2005, in which it stated in the executive summary:

'The scope of private ownership [in China] has become substantial, producing well over half of GDP and an overwhelming share of exports. Private

companies generate most new jobs and are improving the productivity and profitability of the whole economy. The government has restructured the state owned business sector, resulting in a massive loss of jobs. Still, a large part of the state sector remains to be restructured; policies to facilitate this process have been identified and are being expanded. [4]

The significance of embracing the non-state sector and its role in economic growth will be discussed later in this chapter.

The Impact of Entry to the World Trade Organisation 2001

China entered the World Trade Organisation (WTO) after 14 years of negotiations in late 2001. Initial assessments of the risks of China's entry were that it would present huge challenges, and expose China's financial services industry and its agricultural sector in particular to major competition especially from multi-national organizations. At the time, a number of commentaries appeared in publications like the Economist, saying that while the rewards of signing up to a global rules based system would bring great benefits to China, there were also real issues about how it might be able to fulfill its obligations within the time frames stipulated in the agreement. The political importance of entry to an international organization like the WTO, along with other macro-economic surveillance regulations from the International Monetary Fund (IMF) or the World Bank was that they allowed Chinese leaders to bring

---

4. OECD 2005, Executive Summary

about changes domestically which would have been difficult without these external commitments. In that sense, as one study of China's internationalization argues, officials use 'international institutions to overcome domestic resistance to reform'. [5]

WTO entry for Shanghai was particularly important because of the large parts of the agreement that covered the financial services sector. This will be covered in more detail in the next chapter. However, as one academic in Shanghai during interviews in November 2012 commented, the objective of building Shanghai as a financial centre was already articulated at the 14th Party Congress in 1992. Entry to WTO only deepened this commitment, just as it impacted on the rest of the Chinese economy by showing a clear strategic emphasis on internationalization and to integrating and engaging with the global economy. That the city took entry into WTO seriously in terms of how they assessed its likely impact on the local economy is made clear from the fact that the Development Research Centre of the Shanghai Municipal People's Government, the Shanghai Planning Commission, the Shanghai Economy Commission and the Shanghai Foreign Relations and Trade Commission all supported the establishment, on 26th October 2000, of a Shanghai WTO Affairs Consultation Centre. [6] 'It was decided at the start that, constitutionally, the Centre's main functions would be to provide training, information, study and legal aid services which are related to WTO affairs' so that governments and companies would be able to 'familiarize themselves with and to adopt practices that are in accordance with WTO rules.' In this context, setting up such a specific organization focused on understanding entry to WTO was motivated by a vision where WTO entry would be 'the new driving force behind Shanghai's endeavor to turn itself into "one dragon head and three centres" and provide the city with greater room for growth in the world.' [7]

---

5. Rosemary Foot; Andrew Walter. *China, the United States and the Global Order*. Cambridge University Press, Cambridge, 2011, p.265.
6. Peter Gallagher; Patrick Low; Andrew L Stoler. *Managing the Challenges of WTO Participation: 45 Case Studies*. Cambridge University Press, Cambridge, 2005, p.170.
7. Ibid.

And entry to WTO, as many of the statistics already quoted in this chapter show, did compliment in particular the process of internationalization on which the city and country had embarked. The economic crisis from 2008 that beset developed economies and had such an immediate effect on China's exports only underlined how much China needed now to calibrate its engagement strategy. The crisis from late 2007, and the collapse of exports through markets dying up in developing countries in 2008 and 2009, only underlined a trend that had began to appear much earlier – what economists Mauro Guillen and Emilio Ontiveros call the 'turning point' where productivity is now shifting towards emerging markets.[8] The export orientated model from 1978 on which so much growth has been built in China is now changing, with a shift towards China being its own consumption market, but also a destination for increasing amounts of capital. This reinforces the need for Shanghai to be a financial centre, and operate as an interface between China and the outside world.

For enterprises, the crisis from 2008 only deepened the need for internationalization of domestic enterprises. Guillen and Ontiveros point out the rise of emerging market companies as multi national actors, with increasing numbers in the lists of world's largest firms. 'A quarter of the largest firms in the world, 29 per cent of the total number of multinational firms and 41 per cent of new foreign direct investment flows originate from emerging and developing economies.'[9] Chinese enterprises account for a large amount in each of these areas. The WTO entry underlined the commitment to marketisation, and to the shift from industry to service sector in the city, with a need for the businesses in the financial services sector based there to meet international standards. But WTO entry also created space for a deepening commitment to engaging with inward investment, and, more recently, to supporting enterprises in the city becoming outward investors. These were national trends, but ones which were Shanghai

---

8. Mauro F. Guillen; Emilio Ontiveros. *Global Turning Points: Understanding the Challenges for Businesses in the 21st Century*. Cambridge University Press, Cambridge, 2012.
9. Ibid., p.41.

The Shanghai Economy

was at forefront of and managed to develop more quickly. In that sense, WTO only solidified Shanghai's role as an national economic incubator.

The Role of International Trade: Imports and Exports

Shanghai is one of the world's great ports. It took in and exports 12 per cent of China's trade in 2011. In 2010, Shanghai took over Singapore to be the world's busiest container port, handling 29 million TEUS (Twenty-foot equivalent Unit), a figure that increased to a global high of 30 million in 2011. Located in five areas, the deepest is the Yangshan deepwater port able to take the largest container vessels, where construction finished in 2005. The trade that moves through this port reached USD 312 billion of imports in 2011, from USD 8 billion two decades before, and USD499 billion of exports, up from USD 8 billion in 1990. This statistic more than any other illustrates the remarkable growth of internationalization over the period since the city was made a special economic zone. In fact, the figures for imports and exports map out perfectly the liberation of productive forces since entry to WTO in 2001:

Table: Shanghai Export and Import Figures from its Ports, 1990-2011

Year	Exports value, billions of USD	Imports value, billions of USD
1990	8.6	8.6
1995	25.6	22.5
2000	61.5	47.7
2001	68.0	52.4

143

2002	81.8	60.6
2003	112.3	88.8
2004	161.2	121.3
2005	212.4	138.2
2006	266.5	162.1
2007	328.4	192.4
2008	393.6	212.9
2009	325.1	190.3
2010	423.3	261.3
2011	499.9	312.3

These figures map a number of major stories, and show how Shanghai is positioned at the face between China and the world's economies. The first story is the initial liberation of productive forces in 1990 when the city became a special economic zone. This saw the tripling of the value of goods imported and exported, although the amounts for both remained about the same until 2000, when exports started to outstrip imports by over a third. Entry to the WTO in 2001 only reinforced and accelerated this trend, as China became the major manufacturing power in the world. From 2001 to 2006, in the period in which China implemented the commitments it had signed up to in November 2001, exports rose fourfold, while imports only doubled. In 2008, the impact of the global economic crisis saw the first falls in 15 years to the figures. But this also saw a readjustment, with the import figures growing more strongly proportionally after the crisis than export figures.

Goods from Shanghai are exported mainly within the Pacific region. The largest single destination for exported goods, making up nearly a third of the 2011 total, is the United States, to whom Shanghai exports USD 147 billion of goods. Hong Kong Special Administrative Region comes in at a sixth of this (USD 24.9 billion). In terms of imports, the largest in 2011 was from Japan (USD 53.9 billion), Germany (USD 31 billion), the United States (USD 30 billion) and South Korea (USD 28.3 billion).

In terms of the structure of exports from Shanghai, electromechanical goods were the largest group, with USD 148 billion in 2011. The second highest were high tech products, with USD 93 billion.

Shipping in the Shanghai Economy

In 1995, the then President Jiang Zemin said that Shanghai should be a shipping centre, making it one of the priorities for the city's development plan. This was logical. The city after all had a superb location, at the confluence of major rivers, with a vast hinterland it could service logistically behind it, and the easiest routes to countries which were major trading partners like South Korea, Japan, and the United States. Trade relies on shipping, with 90 per cent of global trade flows being moved by water. A road network would be unable to take such vast volumes of goods. According to an official at the Shanghai Shipping Exchange, a ship with ten thousand tones only needs 20 workers, and is less environmentally damaging than air or road. Economically and environmentally, therefore, shipping makes sense. Road development is less environmentally friendly, but also uses up precious land resources.

Shipping is also linked intimately to finance. The earlier bonds, banks and stock markets were reliant on ships and the goods they brought or sent. In the 1980s, Shanghai's shipping was highly local. It serviced mainly domestic needs. There was little competition and little impetus to develop. But entry to WTO also meant opening up of the shipping sector. It was particularly important because of the imminent increase in trade flow amounts, and the lack of proper road infrastructure to service these domestically.

What was important was that the opening up the sensitive shipping sector was controlled and planned. The Baltic Exchange in London had been in existence over two and a half centuries, supplying finance to build ships and ports. For Shanghai to have the same kind of facility, it needed both the software and hardware to achieve this. There was need both for the production of ships, for the development of the port, but also for the creation of new insurance, credit and banking services which were derived from this new development. The ambition of the city in 2001, however, was to be the global shipping centre. This was a natural corollary from its development in manufacturing. With the opening of the Yangshan deepwater port Shanghai was able to service not just the neighboring provinces, but also major industrial centres like Chongqing and Wuhan, further inland into China.

One of the most important assets that the port and shipping sector in China share, and in which it parallels the finance sector, is that Shanghai has a potential reach over a country with 1.3 billion people – something that differentiates it sharply from Singapore, the previous holder of the world's busiest port title before 2009, and Hong Kong, where custom barriers still exist under the One Country Two Systems arrangement put in place when the territory reverted to Chinese sovereignty in 1997.

Shipping remains critical for Shanghai's growth into the future. It also assists in the development of the finance sector. Shipping demands excellent human capital, and modern management techniques. The objective of the port and shipping sector in Shanghai by 2020 therefore is to be a shipping centre with excellent human capital, supporting associated industries, and assisting in the city's vision of its continuing internationalization. One of the great challenges here is that taxes remain relatively high, as they are set in Beijing rather than locally, meaning that it is more expensive for tariffs for some goods to come here than competitors like Hong Kong. The other great challenge is towards the environment, for although the largest ships are kept away from the key residential areas of the city, they are still producers of some pollution.

Agriculture

Shanghai, despite intense urbanization, still has an agricultural sector. As with most of China before 1980, the largest employer and the largest sector in the economy was agricultural production, and even now the city has some agricultural capacity left. In 2011, according to the Information Office of the Municipal City Government, the sector produced RMB 12.49 billion of goods, down 0.7 per cent on 2010. Agricultural output reached RMB 31.41 billion, with the main areas being forestry, livestock and fisheries. The city also exported agricultural products, with over 2200 certified farm products, exporting RMB 1.26 billion of agricultural goods. Perhaps surprisingly, Shanghai has over 86 thousand hectares of modern crop land, and 13 thousand growing vegetables along with 170 livestock farms. Even so, this was inadequate for feeding a city of over 24 million people which was increasing its population by half a million a year. Shanghai has a food security issue. 97 per cent of its food is imported, with major supplies coming from Heilongjiang province where the city had supply deals with important farms and Anhui. Neighbouring provinces such as Zhejiang and Jiangsu also provide food stuffs.

IT

In terms of the Information Technology (IT) sector, this has figured as one of the major sectoral priorities for the city in the last decade. In 2011, the added value from the IT sector increased 11 per cent over the previous year. Added value from IT services came to 110 billion yuan, up 17 per cent on the previous year. Expenditure on research and development in the IT sector has increased alongside this, with a doubling over the decade from 2000 of science and technology institutions, and an increase in 190 thousand people involved in scientific research in 1990 to 370 thousand in 2011. The most startling indication of how important the IT sector figures in the economy of the city is in the increase in production value of new products in this area from 140 billion yuan in 2000 to 714 billion in 2011, with sales revenues also rising from 139 billion yuan to 777 billion in the same period. Patent applications have risen from 11 thousand to 80 thousand per year. The city has increased its investments in IT infrastructure up to 2.6 per cent of the whole fixed asset investment figure.

Property

When I first visited China and lived here in the mid 1990s, the vast majority of Chinese lived in the work units in which they worked, with houses allocated to them and strict rules on how much space they had, and how many rooms. The houses I visited at that time were all compact, some of them nicely furnished and decorated, but almost none were villa style house, with the only relatively large buildings being courtyard houses in the countryside. Since then, the work unit system has largely been dismantled. People are free to save and buy their own house. In Shanghai, large new apartments and villas are being constructed almost weekly. This is a sign of the changing times over the last two decades.

Property ownership is one of the most crucial issues for building a middle class, stakeholder society. The property market in Shanghai is therefore vital for the development of the city. It is an integral part of the economy, and one of the key elements for social cohesion. For the last few years since 2005, however, there have been constant issues about the heating up of property prices and the possibility of a property bubble. According to the Shanghai Daily, in 2012 average prices in Shanghai for residential homes rose to a record, with prices climbing 3.6 per cent over the previous year. An increase in already built homes meant that the sale of pre-owned homes rose by 50 per cent.[10]

In recent years the property market has seen numerous attempts to cool it down, from restricting the number of homes one person can buy to putting limits on unmarried people being home owners. According to the Wall Street Journal, the number of apartments built in Shanghai alone in the last decade 'would fill more than 800 empire state buildings.' Despite this, the amount of residential space per capita is small – only 17 square metres.[11] High prices for property also cause problems, with the average price for the first half of 2012 of homes being RMB 22 thousand per square meter, meaning that home ownership in Shanghai is the lowest amongst China's largest forty cities. Property is still simply too expensive in the city for the average resident. In the last decade, home prices in the city had tripled in value.

The commercial market is similarly explosive. According to the People's Daily Online, investments in office buildings and retail properties grew 43.4 per cent and 34.2 per cent year on year in

---

10. *Shanghai Daily*, 9 June 2013, p.9.
11. James T. Areddy. 'In Shanghai, High Prices Keep Lid on Real-Estate Stimulus'. *Wall Street Journal*, 1 August 2012.

the first quarter of 2012, outpacing the 19 per cent growth in investment in residential property. The report cited the example of an investment firm buying a commercial property in Shanghai's suburbs in June 2012, which was 425 per cent more than the property's offer price. 'The government', the report stated, 'needs to strengthen its supervision in the commercial property market and issue policies to curb irrational investment. For example, it should lift risk weighting on loans for commercial property development to discourage banks from financing such projects.'[12]

Property ownership and land utilization and development however are critical factors for Shanghai's vision of its future. From 2000 to 2011, the amount of area constructed in the city by real estate agents rose from 552 million square feet to 1.2 billion. Two thirds of these figures were for residential properties. The value of the buildings completed tripled, along with the average construction costs. Investment amounts in the real estate market rose fourfold.

Foreign Direct Investment in Shanghai

Foreign Direct Investment (FDI) has, since 1979 and the passing of the first national joint venture law allowing capital into China, been one of the most important engines of technology transfer, expertise inflow and supply of capital behind GDP growth. The importance of FDI in Shanghai's growth has never been disputed.

Shanghai before 1949 saw some of the earliest foreign companies

---

12. Yu Fenghui, 'Commercial Property Market a Bubble Waiting to Explode', People's Daily Online, 13 July 2012.

coming to China. Standard Chartered the bank, and Shell, the petroleum company, were active in the city in the 19th century. Shell maintained a presence there from 1949, although this was disrupted by the Cultural Revolution (1966-1976). From 1980, however, the city has seen an explosion of foreign companies moving there, with the European Chamber of Commerce reporting that of its 1700 member companies registered nationally, the largest group were in Shanghai in 2012. In the last decade, the number of signed contracts by foreign enterprises in Shanghai has almost tripled, rising from 1814 signed in 2000, to 4329 for 2011. By 2011, there were a total of 63,826 signed contracts in Shanghai, of which over 17 thousand were in traditional joint ventures between foreign partners and local ones, 5 thousand were cooperative ventures, and 41 thousand solely owned foreign ventures, something which had been allowed since the early 2000s. This figure was just under 8 per cent of the total signed contracts for the whole of China. In terms of the sectors that this money goes into, 300 of the signed contracts were in primary industries, 25 thousand in secondary industries (the vast bulk of this in industry and manufacturing) and 25 thousand in tertiary industries. Tertiary industry, however, was becoming overwhelmingly the favourite sector in which to invest, with 4057 of the 4329 signed contracts made in 2011 being in that area. By the end of 2011, the contractual amount of FDI in Shanghai was USD 195.22 billion, with the actual amount coming in at USD 119.02 billion. Wholly owned foreign enterprises made up three quarters of this figure. Shanghai is therefore seen as an important place for companies from abroad to come and run their enterprises independently. Despite the fall in levels of foreign investment in China nationally in 2012, Shanghai's financial services and the number of companies headquartered in the city meant that it was able to see a record increase of FDI in 2012, seeing the amount rise by USD 15 billion over the course of the year, an increase of 20.5 per cent from 2011, compared to a 3.6 decline in the rest of the country. This made it rank 25th globally amongst financial centers in attracting FDI, according to global accountancy firm Price Waterhouse Coopers. 'Investment in the service industries made up 83.5 percent of the city's total FDI, highlighting the city's enhanced economic focus on the services sector,' the Shanghai Municipal Commission of Commerce stated on the 1st January 2013.[13]

One of the expectations of China's entry into WTO was precisely that it would mean more companies coming to invest. But the vast bulk of this investment still comes from Hong Kong, Japan, or Taiwan. For Shanghai, the top ten investment regions into the city's economy are listed below. Hong Kong makes up almost a third of the contractual and actual cumulative amount, and has maintained this commitment into 2011, when it made 1448 of the 4329 signings for new investment that year.

Table: Foreign Direct Investment Into Shanghai 2011: Regional Origin

Country or region	2011 number of contracts signed that year	Cumulative total by the end of 2011 of contracts signed	Cumulative total of contracted foreign investment by end 2011 (Billion USD)	Cumulative total of actual FDI by the end of 2011 (Billion USD)
Hong Kong SAR	1448	19182	69.4	36.7
Japan	645	8800	19.9	14.3
USA	318	6940	14.8	9.2
Singapore	207	3278	12.0	6.7
Germany	147	1514	7.34	5.28
Taiwan	386	6950	5.83	3.85
United Kingdom	74	1047	2.77	2.23

---

13. 'Foreign Investment Record as Shanghai Bucks National Trend'. *Shanghai Daily*, January 2013, p.A3.

France	59	668	2.77	1.69
South Korea	213	2288	2.73	1.53
Australia	57	1136	1.19	0.6

Source: Shanghai Municipal Commission of Commerce

In all, Shanghai had investment from 151 countries and regions by the end of 2011, with 353 multinational corporations setting up their regional headquarters in the city.

Retail and Foreign Investment

If Shanghai is a city in which consumption is increasing, then one of the key investment areas for foreign companies must be in retail. After all, since the global economic crisis set in late 2007, the expectations of most businesses and economists is that consumption will be driven by the emerging markets in China and India, where there has been sustained high growth over much of the last decade. Consumption is low as a proportion of GDP in China – coming in at just under a third, whereas capital investment remains high. The structural readjustment would see this change, with consumption creeping up to levels similar to developed countries like the UK and the USA where it constitutes almost two thirds of GDP. But retail is a notoriously difficult sector, as companies like Wal-Mart, Tesco and Marks and Spencer's have discovered during their forays abroad. Marks and Spencer's in particular set up in Shanghai in the early 2000s, only to find the market here too tough. They have since scaled back their China presence. B&Q, the British home decoration retailer, radically changed their business model in order to operate in China, opening three shops in the early 2000s, which initially did very successfully. In the UK, B&Q operate a 'do it yourself' business, due to the relatively high level of labour costs. People simply go and buy the materials they need and then do the work themselves in their own homes. But in China, at least until the late 2000s labour costs were cheap, and housing stock relatively new. In this context, simply going to a store, choosing the home décor and then having a company come and fit out the new apartment was more popular. By 2010, however, B&Q had found business far tougher and their stores were scaled back. Consumer mood was changing, and the company had trouble catching up.

For food and general retailing, things are even tougher. In 2012, there was a slow-down of growth in the city's retail sector, largely brought about by consumer cautiousness. The uncertainty in the international economic situation and the impact this was having on growth in China had percolated through to households, who were being more careful how they spent. Carrefour, the French retailer, who have been present in China since 1991, has 24 stores in the city out of a total of 212 in the whole country. Shanghai's average store turnover reveals how competitive the city is, and how tough its consumers are to please. The average Shanghainese tend to like imported food, and are easier to accept new ideas about what to eat of how food can be presented than in other locations in China. The things they most want are high value and safety. The yield from Beijing stores is higher, despite have four fewer shops. Carrefour in Shanghai has a high number of individual shoppers, but a lower spend per person.

For Carrefour, 70 per cent of their products are in food, and the remainder consists of other goods like clothing or household goods. For retailers, they have to concentrate on service to maintain customer loyalty. They are also dependent on a good supply chain. They have to walk a path between being innovative and finding new products, but also not alienating their customer base with things that are disruptive. Concerns about intellectual property rights protection mean that innovation is always risky. Ideas can be easily copied. This is a shared problem between foreign and local companies.

In the retail sector, by 2020, despite the doubling of the city's per capita GDP, and the rise of people's spending power, cautiousness in spending habits are unlikely to change. Labour costs will rise in the next decade. Retail in particular is in the service sector, and is dependent on people. This means that labour costs will have a direct impact on the competitiveness of the company. It is likely by 2020 that high end stores and the local corner shops will continue to thrive, as these key into the new social configuration of the city. Localization and the location of shops will continue to be critical, with retail and commercial land prices expected to continue to be high over the next decade.

The rise of internet business is one key area for development. Carrefour, Wal-Mart and Tesco have so far all experimented in this area, but with limited success. There is a need for good logistics, more people using credit cards or secure online payment methods, and better online technology. But this is likely to develop fast, and by 2020 the city is likely to see a thriving online business environment. Credit card payments are already increasing instore, although the charges paid by the main credit card supply companies are still too high. These are likely to come down in the next decade.

Carrefour employs four thousand people in Shanghai, from a total of 45 thousand in the whole of China. The biggest retailer is RT-Mart (Taiwan), with Wal-Mart next with 30 stores in the city, and Tesco with 25. Carrefour currently comes fourth. As a testament to the complexity of the city's demographics, in four of Carrefour stores foreign customers are more numerous than local ones. For retailers, one of the key challenges for their work in the next decade will be supporting environmental sustainability, and continuing to find well qualified people to employ — something that is becoming increasingly difficult as the labour market gets more competitive. Sourcing goods locally will also continue to be challenging, as will ensuring food and product safety and protecting intellectual property.

■■■■■■■■■■■■■■■■■■■■■■

One of the longest established foreign businesses in the city has been Shell, who started importing oil from East Asia in 1889, 22 years before the end of the Qing Dynasty. In 1894, Shell began importing kerosene from Hong Kong to Shanghai, and maintained operations in the city throughout the Sino Japanese war, only ceasing when its businesses in Hong Kong and Shanghai were taken by the Japanese in 1941. From 1949 and the establishment of the People's Republic of China, Shell became the only foreign oil company trading in China. After a brief closure of its offices in Shanghai during the Cultural Revolution, where they were located along the Bund, the company attended the Guangzhou Trade Fair in 1970, and reopened its office in the city in 1978, establishing its first joint venture in 1982 and signing a major deal with Sinopec and China National Overseas Oil Corporation (CNOOC) for USD 4.2 billion in 2000.[14]

A second good example of foreign investment which is in Shanghai is the Shanghai Yaohua Pilkington Glass Group, established as a joint venture in 1983, and becoming one of the first listed manufacturers in China after listing on the Shanghai stock exchange in 1993. By 2010, the company had assets of RMB 6.4 billion, and sales of over RMB 2.6 billion. The company's glass can be seen throughout the city, covering in particular the Shanghai World Financial Centre. But it is also used in buildings like the New Tokyo Tower in Japan, the German Frankfurt AirRail Centre, Hong Kong's international

---

14. Kerry Brown. *The Rise of the Dragon: Inward and Outward Investment in the Reform Period, 1978-2007*. Chandos Publishing, Oxford, 2008, pp.99-100.

commercial centre and the Californian Academy of Science in San Francisco. The company also makes glass for cars.

European Companies in Shanghai – Why They Are There, and What Do They Want?

Europe is one of China's largest trading partners, in terms of imports and exports. It also has significant amounts of foreign investment and representation in China, where it runs seven Chamber of Commerce offices representing companies. The largest of these is in Shanghai. Here, the Chamber focuses on lobbying through working groups, particularly on market access where it wishes to see increased ability to sell to the rising number of increasingly wealthy consumers in the city. The largest such working group is the Banking one, with between 40 to 50 members, including companies like HSBC, Standard Chartered, Citi, and the Bank of East Asia. For the EU, banking is regarded as a sectoral strength, despite the crisis from 2008.

In the annual business confidence survey that the EU Chamber of Commerce undertakes, it was found that 25 per cent of the companies were considering moving more capacity to China in 2012. However, China was losing its low cost advantage. A new trend (see below) was increasing numbers of Chinese companies looking to go to Europe to invest or set up offices. The EU Chamber of Commerce for its members sees this process of outward Chinese investment into Europe as a major possible route for opening up the domestic market.

Shanghai Outward Investment

Since the late 1990s, the Chinese government has supported a process of Chinese companies 'going out'. The motives behind this were complicated. The key issue was that in an era in which China's economy was integrating more deeply into the global one, there was now a need for companies which were able to operate more globally. One very practical issue was that as Chinese manufacturing expanded, the key enterprises which were part of this supply chain needed to set up service networks in their key markets, particularly in Europe and North America. A second issue was the need to secure access to resources, and energy, with the three large state energy companies, Sinochem, Petrochina and the China National Overseas Oil Corporation (CNOOC) becoming very active in the Middle East, in Africa and in Latin America in particular. By 2011, Chinese enterprises had become increasingly interested in investing abroad, with more figuring the Forbes list of global companies, and greater brand recognition.

According to the Ministry of Commerce Annual Statistical Bulletin of China's Outward Foreign Direct Investment, by the end of 2010 China's outward FDI net flows reached USD 68.81 billion that year, up 21 per cent on the year before. By the end of 2010, more than 13 thousand Chinese companies had 16,000 overseas enterprises in 178 countries. China's net stock of FDI had reached USD 317 billion, which, according to the United Nations Conference on Trade and Development (UNCTAD) stood at 5.2 per cent of the FDI global flow that year, and 1.6 per cent of the global accumulated stock by the end of 2010. From 2002, therefore, when China had a stock of only USD 29 billion of FDI, by 2010 this had increased more than ten fold. [15]

---

15. MOFCOM, '2010 Statistical Bulletin of China's Outward Foreign Direct Investment.'

Shanghai's role in this was important, as its enterprises were key ones in the go global strategy. Of the top five provinces, cities and autonomous regions with stocks of investment abroad by 2010, Shanghai had become the second strongest after Guangdong.

Table: China's Top Five Provinces or Cities for Outward FDI by Stock 2005-2010 (Non Finance)

Province	2005 (USD billions)	2010 (USD billions)
Guangdong	3.18	11.62
Shanghai	1.84	6.09
Zhejiang	0.40	5.84
Shandong	0.67	4.95
Beijing	0.92	4.8

Source: MOFCOM

Between 2005 and 2010, the rise was exponential:

Table: China's Top Five Provinces in Terms of Outward FDI Flows Non Finance 2005-2010

Province	2005 (USD millions)	2010 (USD millions)
Zhejiang	158.17	2679.15
Liaoning	30.19	1935.66
Shandong	159.04	1890.01
Guangdong	207.08	1599.77
Shanghai	159.04	1584.68

By the end of 2011, there were a total of 1680 enterprises from Shanghai active abroad, a rise of 172 on the previous year, with an investment value of USD 10.34 billion, a rise of 25 per cent over the previous year.

China (Shanghai) Pilot Free Trade Zone

On September 29, 2013 the Shanghai Pilot Free Trade Zone was officially set up with the approval of the State Council. Premier Li Keqiang assented to this approval, and called this resolution an attempt to "explore a new path and a new mode of opening up to the outside world."

The Free Trade Zone (FTZ) is about 28 sq km, covering the Waigaoqiao Free Trade Zone, Waigaoqiao Bonded Logistics Park, Yangshan Free Trade Port Area and Shanghai Pudong Airport Comprehensive Free Trade Zone. It is the first zone of its kind in China, with Tianjin and Xiamen soon to follow suit.

Why has China set up the Shanghai Pilot Free Trade Zone?

The establishment of the Shanghai Pilot Free Trade Zone reminds people of the special economic zones set up in Shenzhen and other coastal areas over 30 years ago, which brought about leapfrog development for the local economy and society, and stimulated economic development across the country. This pattern, in which once some experimental policies and institutional reforms adopted in certain areas work well they will be introduced to other and larger areas, has proved effective in China. This indicates that the Chinese government's intention is to try first and then popularize. In this sense, the establishment of the Shanghai Pilot Free Trade Zone is significant.

According to a report in the *People's Daily* on August 23, the second day after the State Council's approval, Xiao Lin, president of the Shanghai Academy of Development and Reform said that he believed this is an innovation made by China to advance reform and opening up at a higher level in the new historical conditions, to cater to national strategy and new trends in economic globalization.

This report made specific mention of exploring a negative list management approach to gradually form investment rules in accordance with international practices through establishing the Shanghai Free Trade Zone, and to reach a higher standard in trade and investment liberalization, and put more stress on fair competition and rights protection.

More importantly, the Shanghai Free Trade Zone will play an exemplary role in economic upgrading for other areas in China. The central government is expecting it to take the lead in practicing international rules, legal norms, government services and operation pattern, and to provide a testing ground and new feasibility mode to deepen reform and opening up across the country.

The Shanghai FTZ's significance for the world

The establishment of the Shanghai Pilot Free Trade Zone has far-reaching significance for the world economic landscape. First, it means there will emerge a most competitive international financial and logistics center in the Far East. Shanghai will thus integrate more with the outside world, and, together with Hong Kong, form one of the "twin engines" of the Chinese economy. In particular, prospects are good for RMB convertibility. The Shanghai FTZ's growing advantages in finance and logistics will have an impact on some other important financial and logistics centers in Asia such as Singapore and Tokyo.

An article in *The Washington Post* in August focused on the significance of the zone in the sphere of finance: 'The zone could allow for a loosening of capital controls and flow of private capital into the banking sector, while supporting Shanghai's ambitions to become a global financial center.' *The New York Times* remarked that the Shanghai FTZ is signaling financial reform, and will become a bridgehead for the loosening of capital control and RMB convertibility. *The Economist* commented, 'The Shanghai FTZ will help boost China's efforts to become a pan-Asian supply chain hub... and could also allow Shanghai to develop world-leading commodities exchanges.'

Second, the Shanghai FTZ will attract more foreign-funded enterprises with its institutional superiority and preferential policies. The zone has created a highly open and relaxed investment and business environment in terms of market access, national treatment, business operations and investment services based on international standards. Citibank and DBS (Development Bank of Singapore) have been the first among foreign banks to locate in the zone.

Institutional innovation—overall plan for the China (Shanghai) Pilot Free Trade Zone

The Chinese government has stressed that the establishment of this zone is not only a preferential policy but also an innovation and institutional reform.

The Overall Plan for the Shanghai Pilot Free Trade Zone issued on September 27 makes it clear that the reform measures highlight the following six areas: financial services; shipping and logistics; commercial trade; professional services such as law and engineering; culture and entertainment; and social services.

In the areas of financial services, the reform measures include the following: Qualified foreign financial institutions will be allowed to set up foreign banks; qualified private capital and foreign financial institutions will be allowed to establish joint-venture banks and restricted-license banks; and qualified Chinese banks will be allowed to conduct offshore business.

In shipping services, the reform measures relax the restrictions on the proportion of foreign equities in joint-venture international shipping enterprises, and the transport administration authorities of the State Council will be in charge of rule making; foreign ships wholly owned or owned through a holding company by Chinese-invested companies will be allowed to engage in coastal shipping between domestic coastal ports and Shanghai port; and wholly foreign-owned shipping management enterprises may be established in the zone.

In trade and commerce services, foreign enterprises will be allowed to run certain designated telecommunication businesses on the premise of ensuring network information security, and approval of the State Council will be obtained if existing rules are broken; foreign enterprises will also be allowed to produce and sell gaming consoles, and those passing the content examination by the culture authorities will be allowed to be sold in China.

The sectors to be further opened up in professional services include legal services, credit investigation services, travel agencies, human resources agencies, investment management, and engineering design and construction services. The zone will explore mechanisms to enhance cooperation between Chinese and foreign law firms, allow the establishment of foreign investigation enterprises, Sino-foreign joint venture travel agencies, Sino-foreign joint-venture human resources agencies, and joint-stock foreign investment companies. When a wholly foreign-owned construction enterprise contracts a Sino-foreign joint construction project, it will not subject to the restrictions on the investment proportions of Chinese and foreign side.

In cultural services, the zone will cancel the equity caps for foreign performance agencies and allow foreign-owned performance agencies to be established in the zone to provide services in Shanghai; it will also allow wholly foreign-owned entertainment venues to be established to provide services in the zone.

In the field of social services, the FTZ will allow Sino-foreign education and vocational training organizations, as well as wholly foreign-owned healthcare organizations to be established.

Meanwhile, the China Banking Regulatory Commission has issued eight supporting measures, the China Securities Regulatory Commission has issued five supporting measures, and the China Insurance Regulatory Commission has issued eight supporting measures.

Negative List

The FTZ negative list was released on September 30, 2013. The negative list management is also an important approach in the zone. The list specifies the fields and industries which foreigners are not permitted to invest in, but gives domestic and foreign investors the same treatment in areas not covered by the negative list, with foreign investment projects not on the list having to go through the procedure of registration rather than approval. The first negative list details 1,069 subtypes in 18 categories, and applies administrative measures to 190 of them. That is to say, over 80% of foreign investment projects will change from the procedure of approval to registration.

Dai Haibo, deputy secretary-general of the Shanghai municipal government and deputy director of the zone's management committee, said, "The negative list, which is in line with international practice, helps to change the 'hidden rules' into 'well-defined rules', effectively increases administrative transparency, and reduces the administrative cost and possible occurrence of corruption."

Registering a company within four days

The China (Shanghai) Pilot Free Trade Zone soon became the focus of the media after its official launch, and four Wenzhou investors attracted attention after their company became the first one to get a business license in the zone.

Chen Shu, founder of the company, said they submitted the application material on October 8, and completed all procedures — which used to take at least 20 days — in four days.

Another shareholder of the company said that their success was attributable to the zone's policies. On September 29, the first day the FTZ was officially established, the China Insurances Regulatory Commission announced eight supporting measures, to "encourage enterprises to make the best use of both Chinese and foreign resources and markets to realize cross-border financing without restrictions." They came as a foreign-funded company to invest in the insurance sector of China, which is in line with the above-mentioned requirement, and they got their license without any difficulty.

Company registration procedure in the zone: Sign lease contract for the place of registration — apply for company name approval — put lease contract on the record — submit registration material. In the past, companies applying for registration were required to supply loads of documents. Now they need only fill out one form — Investor Registration Application and Letter of Commitment. After the documents are submitted, they will automatically proceed through the whole procedure, saving the applicant the trouble of rushing around.

The major reason for shorter time taken for company registration is that the company shareholders (initiators) shall be responsible for the authenticity and legitimacy of the capital contribution, and shall be liable for the company to the extent of the capital contribution and the shares they have subscribed. The industrial and commercial administration department records the company's registration capital rather than its paid-up capital.

Besides the business license, the company will get a registration certificate, which takes only half an hour. The FTZ practices negative list management for foreign investment, and those sectors not on the negative list need only registration, not approval.

Entry ahead of customs declaration

One example of the conveniences provided in the FTZ is that container cargoes may "enter the zone before making customs declaration." By showing their inward manifest, enterprises may pick up the cargo from the port and ship it to the zone before going through customs formalities. In addition, it is now very easy for enterprises to get the inward manifest. They need only send delivery applications via the customs supervision information system, and will receive the inward manifest in 10 minutes. This customs supervision mode of "entering the zone before making customs declaration" is expected to reduce drastically the time of customs clearance, and consequently the storage fee and logistics cost.

This is called 'making the customs service more flexible', allowing free movement of goods from overseas into the FTZ as well as goods in the FTZ to foreign countries, with little customs supervision. Gu Honghui, deputy director of the Shanghai Municipal Development and Reform Commission, commented, "Allowing more freedom for the movement of goods does not mean a relaxation of control. It is in line with the requirement that the government improve its administration. The emphasis has changed from "examination and approval beforehand" to "supervision afterwards," in order to deliver administrative services with more efficiency.

The Shanghai Pilot Free Trade Zone is working hard to build an information-sharing database covering all enterprises in the zone, covering their basic information, operation and credit, laying a foundation for investment management and comprehensive supervision system innovation. It has also put in place mechanisms for security review, antitrust review assistance and comprehensive evaluation. Enterprise credit is also taken seriously in the zone through the publishing of the corporate annual report — enterprises in the FTZ must deliver individual annual reports to industrial and commercial authorities before a certain deadline and publicize them for public scrutiny.

Xu Bin, a professor of economics and finance and associate dean of China Europe International Business School, commented that the Shanghai FTZ has displayed creativity in government function transformation, and it is highly feasible, applicable and repeatable: "It is expected that in the near future brand-new administration modes such as this will be seen in many places outside the Shanghai FTZ, and bring the government management service mode to a new level." This will also realize the original intention of the central government to the full.

The China (Shanghai) Pilot Free Trade Zone has just been launched, and problems that might affect the foreign-funded enterprises there may crop up. But still we have reasons to wish the best for it.

Shanghai Economy 2020

In the next decade, the Shanghai economy will be at the forefront of the creation of a society in which consumption plays a major role in GDP growth. The city, along with the rest of the country, will see its GDP double over this period. But it will also see the same challenges of governance, addressing inequality, and of building sustainability within the economy as it makes the transition to a developed rather than a developing model. Shanghai will need to upgrade its business through value added – more services, more consumption, more innovation. Policy will need to support this.

Understanding consumption in China is a subject that still mystifies many outsiders. Expectations towards Chinese domestic consumption as an area for growth in the future have been high as other consumption sources have reached saturation point. Looking at consumers in Shanghai gives some concrete insight into what this process will mean for the rest of the country. Here, levels of consumption are high, and increasing. In a study of consumption in modern China, ethnographer Michael B Griffiths argues that 'During the Maoist era (1949-1978) individuality in China was remarkably standardized.'[16] With the reform and opening up, the 'possibilities for self-expression' through consumer behavior have increased. Conspicuous consumption, that is to say 'spending on goods primarily for the purposes of display and prestige' have become much more common. We are entering an era in which our image of the highly standardized 'collective' stereotype of Chinese behavior is shattered by the evidence we see through phenomenon like consumption of great individuality and the values that this promotes. This will be looked at in the final chapter, on culture.

The non-state sector already plays a major role in the configuration of the city's industry. This will increase in the coming decade. The role of the non state as employers, generators of GDP growth, and creators of innovation will increase in the coming decade, and policies will need to be developed to recognize their importance, and to nurture their role. In particular, access to loans will become important, as will more security in terms of the legal environment. In their seminal study of the private sector in China, academics Victor Nee and Sonja Opper state:

> *'In the decades following the start of economic reform in 1978, despite the weakness of formal rules protecting property rights, the private enterprise economy emerged as the fastest growing sector. By 2008, it provided employment for more than 100 million people, roughly twice the size of the workforce employed by all government-owned enterprises. Through bottom-up endogenous processes, entrepreneurs created a parallel*

---

16. Michael B. Griffiths. *Consumers and Individuals in China: Standing Out, Fitting In.* Routledge, London, 2012, p.1.

economy of more than 5.5 million officially registered private firms with more than USD 1.3 trillion of registered capital.' [17]

In their conclusion, they recognize that private enterprises, once they had established their importance in the economy, received recognition from government, through 'business regulation and property protection by enacting laws and regulations designed to secure the political and social legitimacy and legal rights of private businesses.' [18] This process is ongoing, and its importance is in fact increasing. Already, Shanghai enterprises divide equally between state and non state. In terms of efficiency, and in innovation, non state companies are only likely to become more important. State owned enterprises will continue to be important parts of Shanghai's economy, but they will be in capital intensive sectors such as shipbuilding. In terms of sectoral configuration, in the coming decade manufacturing will continue to fall in its contribution to GDP. This will mean that in order to remain globally competitive, manufacturing will need to be upgraded in terms of equipment, management processes, and finance. Capital will need to be used more efficiently (see next chapter). The city government, in its planning, will need to see innovation as not just product innovation but also management and process innovation.

This connects to the second trend which will strengthen in the coming decade – and that is the role of Small and Medium Enterprises (SMEs), the vast majority of which are non state. For these, partnership with foreign enterprises, internationalization, and having an enabling environment to grow are important. In Hong Kong, more than 98 per cent of companies employ less than 20 people. Similar proportions exist in Europe and the US. While the dominance of MNCs and large businesses will continue, with

---

17. Victor Nee; Sonja Opper. *Capitalism from Below: Markets and Institutional Change in China.* Harvard University Press, Cambridge and London, 2012, p.12.
18. Ibid., p.262.

continuing mergers and rationalizations, SMEs will be employers, ways in which people can fulfill their entrepreneurial energies, and significant contributors of taxes and GDP growth. Support in terms of tax relief, access to loans and other benefits will be important. As one foreign enterprise active in Shanghai stated in November 2012, allowing SMEs to be suppliers by giving them better deals to create more competition between them and larger companies is important. SMEs are regarded as loyal, and as good growth partners. Supporting this process in the coming decade will be important. As one senior banker stated in November 2012, 'Shanghai leading the way for the rest of the country in private sector development would be good.' This also addresses some of the research from Yasheng Huang about the continuing role of the state sector and ways in which this sometimes impeded growth in some sectors from his study of Shanghai in 2008.

Shanghai's future is as a city of consumption and services. In that sense, creating a feeling of greater security so that people are able to move from over-saving and under-spending is important. The city has invested hugely in infrastructure. The economic model now needs to move from capital investment to consumption. Private credit will increase, with costs for credit for consumers coming down, and easier access to credit cards. The movement of industry away from the city to inland provinces will continue. This will increase the importance of skilled human capital, and the need for more investment in training and labour skills. It will also mean that the city's pool of labour, skilled or unskilled, is only likely to continue to grow more expensive.

In terms of foreign enterprises, Shanghai will continue to be the destination for most multinational companies wanting to headquarter regionally in China. They will be attracted by stronger signs of good governance, and, like the private sector and SMEs, protection over their property, assets and businesses in the city – and in particular their Intellectual Property Rights (IPR). Tax will be important for foreign enterprises as they come to the city. While they are attracted by the good track record of previous enterprises coming here, their main concern will be about how high taxes are compared to Hong Kong and other cities. They will need to balance the access to a market of 1.3 billion people with the barriers to entry in the city – and in particular issues over market access, over equal treatment for foreign and local enterprises, and over the costs of employment and setting up business. In terms of ease of doing business, Shanghai still ranks relatively low on global scales, behind Singapore and other Asian centres. The city in the next decade will need to reduce bureaucracy for companies, and also address some of the concerns of foreign enterprise in terms of fair treatment for its companies and ability to bid for government procurement contracts according to WTO stipulations. Despite the size of the Chinese economy, EU companies invest more in Kazakhstan than in China. This is an anomaly and needs to change. Foreign enterprises will deepen their technology transfer relationship with partners in Shanghai, and held indigenous businesses.

For multi-nationals, Shanghai must position itself not just as a centre for China, but for the Asia pacific region, leveraging off its excellent logistic and communication links.

In terms of the deeper internationalization of the city's economy and its integration into the region, one key issue will be how Shanghai enterprises go global, and how they relate to the global economy through outward investment. At the moment, the city has few globally recognized brands. Support for its companies prepared for outward investment is important, along with an understanding of the major challenges that companies from China have already experienced in acting abroad. Support should be given by the government to promote state and non-state companies who are ready to internationalise. In particular, Shanghai is likely to see an increasing number of its local companies reach the stage where they can consider international activities to support their sales networks, to seek deeper market access abroad, and to create strategic partnerships for ideas and technology. The city in 2012 will almost certainly see a major increase in its foreign investments. This will have an impact on the culture of local enterprises.

One of the most important challenges is taxes. The city remains uncompetitive in terms of personal and company taxation. This needs to change. Costs of business through taxation are still high.

For the Shanghainese economy, in the coming decade, the most critical issue will be how it leverages its international experience and the openness of the city to deepen this. The decade 2001 to 2011 was dominated by the two events – entry to the World Trade Organisation in 2001 and the impact of the global economic crisis from late 2007. Both of these showed how profoundly the city was linked to global trade flows, and the state of the international economy. In that sense, the issue of internationalization will be an important one to think about. Just as people talk of a China model, they may be tempted to talk of a Shanghai model. But there is much about what the city has done that is unique.

In the journey to create a city with greater services sector and higher consumption, the greatest challenges will be around the sustainability of this model and its internal structure. Shanghai over the period of transition as it doubles its GDP will be under the same strains as the rest of the country. This will create more inequality if systems are not in place to militate against this, either through the tax or social welfare model. There will be a race between wealth creation, but also modes whereby social cohesion can be created and better structures to deliver balance in society. One where some people are clear winners and yet there is also a very visible underclass whose lives have actually worsened in real times would be a huge problem, In that sense, the financial system of the city needs to become rules based, predictable and based on transparency. The sustainability agenda is important. Consumption is good, but there needs to be green consumption, with the public aware of their responsibilities to avoid waste, to buy sustainable products, to eat food from sustainable sources, and to use energy and other public goods efficiently. The public of the city need to be mobilized as much as possible in this great battle to create sustainable high growth.

In the coming decade as this happens, it is clear that the services sector will be critical for the city's future development. At the heart of this is the aspiration to create a global finance centre. It is to that issue that we now turn.

Chapter Six

Shanghai as an International Finance Centre

▲ Brief History

In the 1930s, Shanghai had developed itself into the largest and most influential international financial centre in Asia. Described at the time as a city that was 'bustling with enterprises and some 300,000 foreigners',[1] Shanghai then hosted 24 state banks, 33 foreign banks, and over 200 private lenders and other financial institutions. It also operated one of the world's largest stock markets which came only after New York and London in global rankings.[2]

When China's economic reform took place in 1978, Guangdong was the first province to receive approval from Beijing to develop their own industry and to accept foreign investment. In 1979, four special districts were formally approved to receive the autonomy and granted status as Special Economic Zones. Shanghai because of its entrepreneurial past was another potential site for an experimental zone. However, as was seen in Chapter Two, the city did not do this. This was due mainly to the fact that it was then a heavy tax revenue contributor to the central government. In the words of American political scientist, Ezra Vogel:

---

1. Ezra Vogel. *Deng Xiaoping and the Transformation of China*. The Belknap Press of Harvard University Press, Cambridge, Mass, 2011, pp.394–398.
2. Louise do Rosario. 'Shanghai makes up for lost time'. *The Banker*, 2 March 2003.

'... in 1978, Chinese planners worried that allowing Shanghai to become an experimental zone was too risky. Shanghai was a major Chinese industrial centre and contributed more revenue to the national budget than any other locality, so it would be disastrous for China if Shanghai's industry and revenue streams where to be adversely affected.' [3]

Only from 1990 did the City become a Special Economic Zone.

Over the last three decades, and particular since 1990, Shanghai has embarked on a daunting journey to reclaim its leading position in the financial industry as well as an international financial centre. This was strongly symbolized by Deng Xiaoping's visit to Shanghai in January and February 1991, when the city's potential of becoming an international financial centre was pointed out. [4]

'On January 28, 1991, Deng took his special train to Shanghai where he remained until February 20, taking his winter rest while again trying to light the fire of economic growth. After being briefed by Zhu Rongji, he visited aeronautic and automobile factories and construction site for the Nanpu Bridge, which would soon become the third longest suspension bridge in the world. Deng reiterated what he had said in 1990: that he had made a mistake in not opening up Shanghai in 1979, when he had opened the four SEZs, and that he should have taken advantage of the great intellectual resource of Shanghai. He emphasized the importance of developing Pudong not only for the city itself but for the entire Yangtze River basin. Finance, Deng explained – carefully avoiding using the charged word "capital" – is at the core of a modern economy; if China is to acquire an international status in finance, the entire nation would have to rely on Shanghai'. [5]

---

3. Ezra Vogel. op. cit., p.402.
4. Ezra Vogel. op. cit., p.666.
5. Ezra Vogel. op. cit., p.668.

Not until Deng Xiaoping's Southern Tour a year later in January and February 1992, did Shanghai's opening up and the development of the Pudong area finally receive the official green light for developing a finance market corresponding to the nation's goal for accelerating growth and reform. Thereafter, Shanghai has experienced an impressive double digit growth in GDP with 12% during the period between 1992 and 2011.

Figure 1 shows Shanghai GDP growth rate, which had underperformed the China's overall GDP growth rate before 1992, but outperformed the nation's GDP growth rate since 1992 until 2008.

Figure 1.

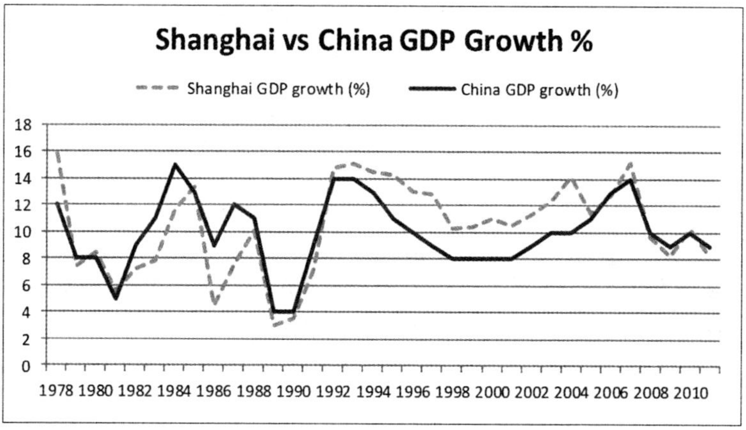

Shanghai vs China GDP Growth %

--- Shanghai GDP growth (%) ▬▬ China GDP growth (%)

Source: *Shanghai Statistical Year Book 2012*, World Bank Statistics Data

On upgrading its industry structure and paving the way for moving to a financial centre, Shanghai has transformed its industry from heavily relying on a manufacturing sector to a more consumption driven economy. Shanghai has thus attracted more foreign investment and become a destination for international brands, multinational companies and foreign financial institutions.

In 1978, Shanghai's service sector accounted for only 18.6% of its

GDP; while its manufacturing sector accounted for as high as 77.4% of GDP. The service sector continued to grow to 36.1% in 1992 while manufacturing fell to 60.8% in 1992. By the end of 2011, Shanghai's service sector climbed to 58% of its GDP; while the manufacturing further declined to 41.3%. (Figure 2)

Figure 2.

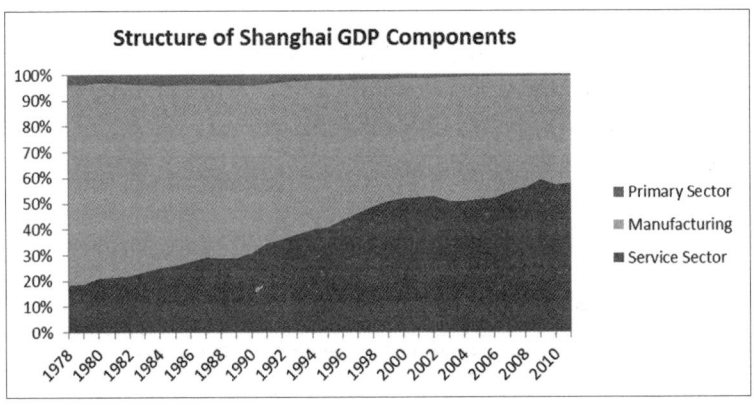

Source: *Shanghai Statistical Year Book 2012*

According to Shanghai Municipality government, Shanghai's GDP reached 2 trillion yuan in 2012, 60% of which was contributed by the service industry.[6] At the same time, Shanghai' financial industry has strengthened its role in the service sector and our data shows the financial sector accounted for more than 20% of the service sector by the end of 2011 and for 11.86% of overall GDP in 2011.

---

6. http://en.shio.gov.cn/presscon/2013/01/29/1152146.html

Development of the Finance Sector

Shanghai's aspirations to become an even more important international finance centre are well known. This determination was addressed by China's State Council in March 2009, with the announcement that the city will become an international financial centre (IFC) by 2020. In the coming decade, if Shanghai is to become a service orientated, highly internationalized middle class consumption driven economy, then the role of the financial services will be critical to this.

The National Development and Reform Commission (NDRC) and the Shanghai Municipal Government have made it clear about their timetable for the development of the city in the next decade in this area. According to a report in the China Daily in January 2012:

> 'China is going to make Shanghai a global financial centre for RMB innovation, transaction, pricing and clearing by 2015. The plan will be part of China's bid to build Shanghai into an international financial centre by 2020 amid a shifting global financial landscape, with China's economic weight and its currency taking a more prominent position on the world stage. The NDRC said in a statement that The 12th Five Year Plan (2011-2015) will be "a period of strategic opportunities" for the construction of the international financial centre'. [7]

Measures include introducing more financial products, gradually opening up the capital market, further financial reform and construction of financial infrastructure. This is in order to increase the scale of the financial market, strengthen the financial service and products, enhance the globalization of Shanghai's in this area, and attracting more foreign financial institutions as well as financial

---

7. Xinhua Agency, 'Shanghai aims to be global financial centre', *China Daily*, 30 January 2012

professionals by a more competitive financial environments.

Statistics over the last decade show just how large this sector has grown. According to the statement announced by the NDRC, the total transaction value of all financial markets in Shanghai has reached 386.2 trillion[8] in 2010 (barring foreign exchange market), a tenfold growth of the amount in 2005, and is due to grow to 1,000 trillion yuan by 2015. Over this period too foreign-funded financial institutions have been encouraged to set up their regional or global headquarters in Shanghai. There were 1,048 financial institutions in the municipal area as of the end of 2011, including 173 foreign ones.[9] 284 thousands financial professionals were working in Shanghai by the end of 2011[10] and 320 thousands financial professionals are due to be employed by 2015, according to the statement.

By 2015, direct financing will account for around 22% of the total social financing in Shanghai (lifted from 16.7% in 2010). The total assets under management will be doubled to 30 trillion yuan over this period from 15 trillion yuan in 2010. Meanwhile, the Shanghai Interbank Offered Rate and RMB central parity rate will become major benchmarks for domestic and foreign RMB asset pricing and transactions. To achieve this, a cross-border RMB investment and financing centre will be established. "Shanghai won't become an international financial centre without the internationalization of RMB, a more open domestic market and more regulated financial system and environment", according to Fang Xinhai, Director General of the office of financial service in the Shanghai Municipal Government (see section below for more on internationalization of RMB).

---

8. Breakdown: RMB 398,396 bn (Shanghai Stock Exchange), RMB 1,234,795 bn (Shanghai Futures Exchange), RMB 410,699 bn (China Financial Futures Exchange), RMB 1,798,225 bn (Interbank Lending and bond market), RMB 20,205 bn (Shanghai Gold Exchange), USD 28.6 bn (Shanghai Diamond Exchange), *Shanghai Statistical Yearbook 2012*. China Statistics Press, Beijing, 2012, p.319.
9. Zhixiong Wang; Junxian Ma. op. cit., p.319.
10. Zhixiong Wang; Junxian Ma. op. cit., p.34.

The Vision for the City's Financial Service

Shanghai has aspired to become a major player in international finance. But it has to compete against Hong Kong, New York, Tokyo and London. The size of their markets is still many times those of Shanghai's however. Despite this, Shanghai is still one of the world's largest stock markets, the Shanghai Stock Exchange, one of the only two stock exchanges operating in mainland China[11], is ranked the fifth largest stock market with a market capitalization of US$2,357bn as of the end of 2011, behind London's US$3,266bn, Tokyo's US$3,325bn, Nasdaq's and New York Stock Exchange's US$4,687bn and US$14,242bn, respectively. However, in terms of trade value, Shanghai is ranked fourth, overtaking London with trade value of US$3,658bn by the end of 2011. However, Shanghai is not an entirely open market to foreign investors due to China's capital control. Hong Kong Stock Exchange is smaller in size with market capitalization of US$2,258bn and trade value of US$1,447bn in 2011.[12] Hong Kong Stock Exchange has about 1,477 listed companies, while Shanghai has 931 listed companies.[13]

Lujiazui, a district in Shanghai, was selected in 2005 to be the only one amongst the 185 state level development zones selected by the State Council in Beijing to specialize in banking and finance. To achieve this, tax benefits were offered. This managed to attract a critical mass of companies to the area. 55 per cent of the office space in Lujiazui was taken by banking and financial users within five years.[14] As of 2012 there are now over 500 overseas financial

---

11. The other one is Shengzhen Stock Exchange, its market capitalization is around US$1,000 bn as of the end of 2011.
12. Data derived from World Stock Exchanges, http://www.world-stock-exchanges.net/top10.html
13. Zhixiong Wang, Junxian Ma. *Shanghai Statistical Yearbook 2012*. China Statistics Press, Beijing, 2012, p.322.
14. *Shanghai Daily*, 14 September 2006

and insurance corporations. By the end of 2012, according to the Shanghai Municipal Department for Foreign Trade and Economic Cooperation, there were 70 financial leasing companies, 50 private equity investment companies, and 10 venture capital companies all active in the banking and finance zone. Of the services sectors (which also included insurance and IT services) finance is particularly significant for Shanghai's internationalization and its definition of how it sees its mediating role between the economies of the rest of China and the outside world.

As shown in the last chapter, it was always envisaged under WTO that Shanghai would be at the forefront of building a financial centre. These ambitions have developed in the last decade with the increase in international activity and the rise in trade volumes. Shanghai aims, according to a senior official in the financial centre, to be not just an offshore centre, like Hong Kong or Singapore, but eventually to become like London and New York as a major centre in its own right, for the simple reason that it has the vast market of the whole of China behind it. For this to be fully realized, the eventual internationalization of the RMB (See below) will be very important. In the future, the RMB is likely to become one of the most frequently used currencies. It's becoming an international currency will be a massive propulsion for Shanghai also becoming an international finance centre. The two are intimately linked.

The main impetus behind Shanghai's fast development so far is the expansion and opening up of the economy throughout China. An increasingly sophisticated domestic economy is demanding more specific products. The financial crisis from 2007 was a big impediment to the development of the financial services sector, pushing back the original plans because of its impact on global finance and banking sectors. But for Shanghai, this crisis was also an opportunity to learn what not to do. China's starting at a different point from other countries meant it could look in particular at what the US or the EU developed economies had done in the financial services sector to understand how it might avoid getting into the same immense problems they suffered from. One of the most important lessons derives from the fact that finance has a lot of externalities. Activity has to be watched, and carefully regulated. A path has to be trod between over regulation and under regulation. It is possible that China currently has too much regulation, but nor does the country have the confidence to completely rely on the market, because of what happened elsewhere in 2007. There is also an issue about the regulators being in Beijing, rather than Shanghai. As the market becomes more developed, it will be necessary for them to be as close as possible to where things are happening.

For those directing the International Finance Centre in Shanghai, there is one strong reason for why people might wish to come to the city – and that is that it is still a place of good profits. If international businesses believe that China will experience good growth in the next decade (and the vast majority do) then the city will become a major centre for finance. The two go hand in hand. If the Chinese economy stagnates or shrinks, then of course there will be immense problems. We have to remember that Shanghai is one amongst a number of possible centres in China, and therefore has to compete not just externally but internally. Its greatest asset internally is the fact that it got off to a head start, commencing the process of internationalizing its finance sector earlier than anywhere else in the country. The main asset externally is that it is the entry point to a huge and expanding economy unlike anywhere else on earth at the moment. The great challenges in developing this sector in the coming decade, beyond the RMB internationalistion, will be opening the capital account, and developing the legal system.

Across all of these challenges, there is the overriding one of the need to continue with reform and internationalization. Shanghai is developing many new products and introducing others that have not been seen in China before. It has a small Futures exchange at the moment, which is government run – there are also bond markets, though the structure of these differ from elsewhere because there are questions about how they are traded in low volumes and on the whole involve the state doing deals with itself rather than a fully open market. The introduction of new products to a more financially sophisticated and understanding middle class population will be critical, but there is a lack of mechanism at the moment for introducing products. In particular the following are major targets:

- To introduce treasury futures

- To reform the stock market

- To reform the Initial Public Offering Process

- To introduce a more market based system.

- To professionalise more quickly and to attract internationally qualified personnel.

The International Financial Centre in Shanghai is a national strategy, with support from the China Regulatory Commission, the central bank, the ministry of finance, and the central government. In that sense, the Shanghai municipal government is one partner in this project.

The Development of Shanghai as an International Finance Centre – the Products

For international banks, Shanghai's development is of major importance. This is the launch place for access to the market in the rest of the country. For banks, the main interest is in the further development of the stock exchange and its internationalization, the need to clamp down on insider trading and deepen the legal infrastructure of the market, and making the stock market more independent. The stock market in Shanghai is highly volatile, with one calculation showing that it delivers no return for 70 per cent of investors, losses for 20 per cent and gains for 10 per cent. From 2000 to 2004 it lost over 50 per cent of its value. In recent years it has continued to be highly volatile.

The key areas for development will be:

- The development of the Shanghai Equity Exchange. This opened on the 15th February 2012 with 19 listings. A report in the People's Daily stated that 'as part of a uniformly regulated over-the-counter market, the exchange will serve as an equity trading platform for high tech start ups and other small and medium sized non public companies based in Shanghai and other regions.' The report continues: 'The exchange will encourage cooperation between start-ups and commercial banks as well as insurance companies, in order to promote the establishment of a diversified financial system in Shanghai.' [15]

- Capital Markets: A report in the Financial Times from 30th January 2012 stated that Shanghai 'intends to expand greatly the size of its capital markets and open them more widely to foreign investors by 2015 as cornerstones in its strategy to become a global financial powerhouse.' According to the report, Shanghai's stock exchange was ranked sixth in terms market capitalization in 2010. According to the Shanghai City Government and the National Development and Reform Commission, Shanghai's interbank bond market was the fifth biggest in the world in 2010, and is likely to be within the top three by 2015. China's derivative market was also aiming to be in the top five by 2015. [16]

---

15. People's Daily Online, 17 February 2012
16. 'Simon Rabonivitch, Shanghai Vows to Expand Capital Markets'. *Financial Times*, 30 January 2012

- Futures Market: regulated by the China Securities Regulatory Commission, this was formed by amalgamating the Shanghai Metal Exchange and the Shanghai Commodity Exchange and Foodstuffs Commodity Exchange in 1999. It deals in futures for copper, aluminum, zinc, natural rubber, and gold. In 2012, for the first time in over half a century, the exchange also began to trade in silver contracts.

- Insurance Market: Wu Dingfu, head of the China Insurance Regulatory Commission (CIRC) stated in 2011 at the National People's Congress that 'setting up an insurance exchange is part of Shanghai's plan to become an international financial centre, which is something the CIRC as a financial regulator, strongly supports.' It is likely the exchange will initially deal in liability insurance, reinsurance, and property and group life insurance products, with risk securitization products, catastrophe bonds and insurance derivatives coming online later. [17]

- Hedge Funds: According to the Wall Street Journal in April 2012, 'Shanghai officials plan to launch a pilot programme that would allow some foreign hedge funds and others to raise yuan funds on the mainland for overseas investment.' [18]

Competition with Hong Kong

As a financial centre, Hong Kong is one of the most important in the world, and is often cited as the place that Shanghai might want to compete with as it continues its own development as an International Financial Centre. Particularly badly hit by the global financial crisis because of the fact that almost 90 per cent of its economic activity

---

17. 'Shanghai Will Pilot Insurance Exchange'. *China Daily*, 7 March 2011.
18. 'Shanghai Cracks Open Door for Hedge Funds'. *Wall Street Journal*, 2 April 2012.

is now in financial services and the service sector, the Special Administrative Region's economy contracted by 2.2 per cent in 2009. It was able to bounce back in 2010 with a 7 per cent growth rate, and in 2012 recorded 3 per cent. In 2010, Hong Kong's stock market was the seventh largest in the world, and the third largest in Asia. By the end of 2010 it had 1352 listed companies with a market capitalization of USD 2.39 trillion. The region also had 146 licensed banks, 23 of them incorporated in the region, and 70 representatives of foreign banks from 22 economies and regions. Hong Kong is one of the leading asset management businesses in Asia, with USD 1 trillion under management by the end of 2009. Hong Kong is the major source of capital flows into the People's Republic of China and the main place in which Chinese state owned companies make their initial listing when internationalizing. In 2007, for instance, PetroChina listed in Shanghai after an initial listing in Hong Kong in 2000. A year earlier, the Industrial and Commercial Bank of China held an IPO which raised nearly USD 22 billion. The Agricultural Bank of China listed in Hong Kong in July 2010 and broke all records with a listed valuation of USD 22.1 billion.

The way in which Hong Kong and Shanghai compete but also leverage off each other has been a perennial source for speculation in the last decade. According to the Financial Times in 2012 'Hong Kong is the city that stands to lose the most from an ascendant Shanghai'. An article by Edgar Cheng, a former Chairman of the Hong Kong Stock Exchange, entitled 'Hong Kong and Shanghai Can Rise Together' produced in 2010 articulates these fears. 'There is a palpable nervousness in Hong Kong these days about the rise of Shanghai. Already the main domestic financial centre in the world's most dynamic economy, Shanghai has an unconcealed aspiration to regain its position on the international stage.' Cheng goes on to argue that in fact Shanghai and Hong Kong can coexist and gain from each other in the years ahead. 'The increased maturity of China's domestic securities market, combined with the huge scale of China's domestic savings, make it natural for Shanghai to become the 'New York of China'. 'Hong Kong should accept this and use it to its advantage.'

The core for this for Cheng is for Hong Kong to innovate in ways in which Shanghai is not able. He cites three areas where Hong Kong can do this:

- Developing RMB denominated financial products, such as RMB denominated bonds (see below), leveraging Hong Kong's role as a buffer zone between China and the outside world.

- Establishing Hong Kong as a risk management centre for the trading of derivative financial products and commodities

- Developing its asset and wealth management capacities.

'These', Cheng concludes, 'are only three of several ways in which Hong Kong can turn China's natural evolution to its advantage. Shanghai's rise, far from threatening its future as a financial centre, should help seal it.' [19] These words echo those of Chen Yuan, then Deputy Governor of the People's Bank of China, who stated in UK in 1996 that Shanghai and Hong Kong could have complementary and mutual reinforcing relationships as financial centres. [20] To underline this, the two signed a Memorandum of Understanding Concerning Advancing Hong Kong-Shanghai Financial Cooperation in 2010, in order to define their involvement with the future internationalization of the RMB (See below). According to the then Secretary for Financial Services and the Treasury K. C. Chan, 'RMB internationalization could not succeed without the support of Shanghai which has the largest pool of onshore liquidity and is the recognized onshore RMB business Centre.' He described Shanghai and Hong Kong as 'twin engines' which are 'in the process of internationalization of China's capital market.'

---

19. Edgar Cheng. 'Hong Kong and Shanghai Can Rise Together'. *Financial Times*, 29 April 2010.
20. For this citation, and for statistics in the opening paragraph of this section, please see Kerry Brown and Sophie Steele, 'Hong Kong in the Global Economy: How the Special Administrative Region Rises to the Challenges Posed by China,' Chatham House Asia Programme Paper ASP PP 2010/05, October 2010, London

Hong Kong continues to have some tangible practical advantages over Shanghai. Its corporate tax rate is a flat 16.5 per cent, compared to over 40 per cent in Shanghai. Personal income tax is also low, at 15 per cent. There are no taxes on dividends, capital gains taxes and inheritance. Import and Export tariffs are also highly competitive (see previous chapter). From February 2010, Hong Kong has announced extensions of tax exemptions for exchange trade funds, tax benefits for bond trading and the promotion of hedge funds by allowing funds domiciled outside Hong Kong but run by residents to qualify to tax exemptions on their profits.

One of the more radical ideas would see Shanghai given a status similar to Hong Kong, as a special region. According to one expert in Shanghai interviewed in November 2012, 'It is very simple. In order to compete with Hong Kong on a totally level playing field, Shanghai must be accorded the same special status. It is a city moving fastest towards the frontiers of China's economy. Waiting for too many approvals can be time consuming and impede the city's competitiveness. In this way, the city could have more powers in setting tax rates, and in attracting international human capital.' In other ways, Shanghai can also position itself as the main portal for the interior in ways in which Hong Kong is not able to. Under the One County Two Systems agreement in 1997, Hong Kong still operates under restrictions in coming into Mainland China. Shanghai can also be a source of human capital for Hong Kong, with greater interchange.

A Tale of Two International Banks in Shanghai

Standard Chartered Bank and the Hong Kong Shanghai Banking Corporation (HSBC) are two global leaders in the banking sector, both of them with strong historic and current links to the city. Their stories map out many of the ways in which Shanghai figured as an important financial centre in the past and how it plans to develop in the future.

Standard Chartered now has 1700 offices in 70 markets globally, with 85 thousand members of staff. Its Shanghai branch was the first to be set up in China in 1858, and it has remained there ever since. According to the company website, 'Standard Chartered Bank (China) Limited is one of the first foreign banks to locally incorporate in China in April 2007.' It now has 23 branches across the country, 75 sub-branches and one village bank. In September 2007 the bank announced the opening of a private bank in Shanghai to serve high net individuals with liquid assets of over USD1 million. Katherine Tsang, the CEO of Standard Chartered Bank (China) stated: 'With the rapid economic growth in China over the past decade, the affluence of the Chinese population has risen significantly. Tapping into the endless opportunities, the newly opened Private Bank in Shanghai will work with the Standard Chartered Bank in Beijing to provide tailor made services for high net worth customers in the nation.'[21]

The Hong Kong Shanghai Banking Corporation, as its name makes clear, is one of the most venerable and longest established international banks with a link to the city. Indeed, as the first chapter described, one of the main buildings along the Bund is named after

---

21. Standard Chartered Bank Press Release, 13 September 2007.

the bank, serving as its headquarters from 1923 to 1955. HSBC was established in Hong Kong in March 1865 and in Shanghai just one month later. Founded by Thomas Sutherland from Scotland, from the time in which it opened in the city it was able to issue locally denominated banknotes. It handled the first public loan in China in 1874. The only pause in HSBC's presence in China was during the Sino Japanese War from 1937 to 1945, but since then it has increased its activities dramatically, buying a 19.9 per cent stake in the Shanghai based Bank of Communications for USD1.75 billion in August 2004. It also has stakes in the Bank of Shanghai, and Ping An Insurance. In 2012, it runs personal and business banking, through HSBC Bank (China) Company Limited which started operations in April 2007 as a wholly foreign owned bank. HSBC now has 143 outlets across China in 45 cities run from the head office in Shanghai, with 28 branches in Beijing, employing over 5000 staff of whom 98 per cent are recruited locally. This is the largest number of outlets and the widest geographical reach of any foreign bank in Mainland China. To the end of 2012, it has invested over USD10 billion in the growth of its operation and financial services in China.

Internationalisation of the RMB

The Chinese RMB is currently a non-convertible currency. It cannot be used to settle invoices or trade internationally, but only within the borders of China. In the last few years, there have been modest moves to make the RMB a more international currency, stemming in part from frustrations from 2008 onwards at the global dependence on the US dollar as the main international currency, followed by the EURO and the Japanese Yen (though here the amounts are far smaller). Making the RMB an international currency would have a dramatic impact on China's capital account and on the flows of capital in and out of the country. But it would also reduce the ways in which the central government would be able to control exchange rates and would remove one of the fundamental tools of fiscal management that they have. For this reason, central government officials have been careful to say that while RMB convertibility is a long term aim, it is not something that is immediately envisaged.

Internationalisation of the RMB would have a massive impact on Shanghai's status as an international finance centre. It would open the financial services sector in the city up radically, and place it at the fore front of one of the great new movements of financial development in the 21st century. In the last few years since 2004 there have been moves largely through the use of Hong Kong to open up modest amounts of RMB business beyond the PRC. In 2004, RMB deposits, remittances, exchange and credit cards were introduced into Hong Kong. In 2005, RMB cheques were introduced. In 2007, there was the introduction of RMB bonds by Mainland banks, and in July 2009 selected companies (retailers, trading companies and banks in Hong Kong and selected regional cities within China) were allowed to open RMB business accounts and transact business in RMB. In June 2010, a trade settlement pilot scheme was introduced.

Hong Kong SAR saw an RMB bond market develop from 2007 with a total of USD 7 billion issued. In 2009, investors were able to access the RMB market in China via the Qualified Foreign Institutional Investors Scheme (QFII). In April 2009 a pilot scheme was introduced where select Chinese enterprises were able to use RMB to settle trade in Hong Kong and other Association of South East Asian Nations (ASEAN) countries. The People's Bank of China, the Minister of Commerce and the Ministry of Finance in Beijing stated that this experiment had been 'smooth, in good order, convenient and popular among enterprises and banks.' In July 2010, it was announced that this scheme would be expanded from two provinces being involved to 20. Even so, the amounts involved were very small. In 2009 USD 2.8 trillion in goods were traded across China's borders. Only USD 10 billion of this amount was settled in RMB denominations. In August 2010, McDonalds restaurants became the first foreign multinational to issue a RMB bond to fund its operations in China.

There is a lively debate about the future development of the internationalization process. For some commentators, expectations should not be too high. According to a report from Deutsche Bank in April 2012, despite the fact that China receives such a large amount of global foreign investments now, 'its currency comprises a mere 0.3 per cent of all global [foreign exchange] turnover.'[22] RMB cross trade business from the PRC into Hong Kong SAR grew to ten per cent of the total trade in 2011, with the expectation of increased demand for RMB financing and loans in 2012. RMB business was expected to deliver lower borrowing costs for companies engaged, minimizing foreign exchange risks, and improving suppliers access. For J. P. Morgan, 'for anyone operating in China, looking to expand in China or working with Chinese entities, the internationalization of the RMB will allow more flexibility in payment, collection and potential investments.' But for other commentators there were more sanguine remarks. Yu Yongding, from the Chinese Academic of Social Sciences, and an advisor to the central government, in a paper published by the Asian Development Bank Institute in July 2012, simply stated that 'the internationalision of the RMB is a major challenge facing the PRC government.... The internationalization of the RMB requires convertibility and liberalization of the capital account. Due to the fragility of the financial system and its lack of attractive financial instruments, the PRC's liberalization of the capital account and hence the internationalization of the RMB must proceed in a gradual fashion.' He continues: 'The PRC's growing economic and trade volumes are favourable conditions for internationalistion. However, other conditions, such as the existence of deep and liquid

---

22. Deutsche Bank, 'At the Centre of RMB Internationalisation: A Brief Guide to Offshore RMB'. April 2012, p.4.

Shanghai 2020

financial markets, have not been met. To create conditions for the internationalization of the RMB, the PRC government should encourage financial markets to play an increasingly important role.'[23]

Challenges for the Future

Douglas J Elliott from the John L Thornton China Centre at Brooking Institute in the US, in a paper discussing how Shanghai planned to build a global financial centre, stated that amongst some of the most important requirements to fulfill this ambition anywhere were 'a very high level of financial expertise, a full range of infrastructure, including globally orientated law firms, a trusted legal system, and connections with a wide range of investors around the world.' [24] In looking at Shanghai compared to other global finance centres, Elliott outlines the following strengths:

- Access to a huge and growing Chinese financial market
- The clear backing of the national and municipal governments
- Existence of futures and options markets
- A vibrant city
- Great progress with hard infrastructure [25]

---

23. Yongding Yu. 'Revisiting the Internationalization of the Yuan'. Asia Development Bank Institute Papers No. 366, 2012/07, pp.23-24.
24. Douglas J Elliott. *Building A Global Financial Center in Shanghai: Observations from Other Centers*. John L Thornton China Center at Brookings, 2011, p.3.
25. Ibid., p.14.

But he also outlined the following weaknesses:

- Limited ability to use sophisticated financial products
- Limited global use of the RMB
- Opaque political decision making processes
- Concern with political favouritism
- Distance from Beijing's financial institutions
- Hesitation about use of Chinese law for global transactions
- Still modest presence of related services
- Further need to develop 'soft' infrastructure more generally. [26]

Despite this list, Elliott concludes that 'Shanghai clearly has a shot at becoming a truly global financial center, but it will make many years of hard work and focused dedication.' According to one senior academic economist based in the city, Shanghai is the only centre in China which has 'the conceptual framework for finance'. It is more westernized, more receptive to outside ideas, and its stock exchange is becoming more standardized. Shanghai has to define itself very clearly as a centre for market transactions, so even foreign banks can locate their marketing departments in the city. For this it needs the total support of the central government in Beijing. The process in becoming a financial centre has been slower than expected, partly due to the financial crisis and the impact of that, and also because of the fact that Shanghai operates with the status of a city. In London, there are over 300 thousand professionals working in the financial services sector. As of 2012, there were fewer than 30 thousand in Shanghai. There is a critical need for more value added in the financial services sector.

There are a number of challenges as the city tries to become a major international finance centre.

---

26. Ibid., p.15.

The first is the issue of corporate governance. Shanghai authorities need to encourage the highest standards of transparency and internal governance for the local and international companies that are based in the city. Corporate governance has become critical since the financial crisis in 2007, in order to restore trust in banks and large financial institutions. Fulfillment of international standards, with rigorous scrutiny, is very important. Observance of the rule of law and strengthened implementation against fraud, malfeasance and corruption are also crucial.

The second is tax. Taxation levels in the city come in at 45 per cent, far higher than in Hong Kong or other centres, impeding on the city's ability to attract international talent. According to one bank in the city, its analysts all prefer to live in Hong Kong because of the lower tax burden there. While tax is set nationally in Beijing, in order to compete fully both for international talent and for business in the future, the City needs some leverage in setting local tax levels so that it can compete more aggressively.

The third is diversifying ownership. This is critical to creating a marketised system. At the moment there are many state owned companies who are partially listed. The role of the state in the market is still profound. Final ownership is still in the hands of government. This has an impact on competitiveness and on the liquidity of the market in Shanghai. A more profound process of marketisation needs to take place.

The fourth is measures to control moral hazard. Because of the final owner being the state, there is a feeling that in the end many of the partially listed companies will never go bankrupt if they become uncompetitive because in the end they will always be bailed out. This 'too big to fail' mentality was one of the largest issues in the global financial crisis from 2007. It was only the collapse of Lehmann Brothers that year that showed that even large financial institutions could collapse, but others were not allowed to go to the wall.

The fifth is payment of dividends. This will become increasingly important. Of the 75 million active accounts on the stock exchange, only a fraction are personal ones. The need to motivate potential investors to see returns on their investment through regular payment of dividends will become more important in getting this number of personal investors up.

The sixth is diversification of products for increasingly demanding consumers with a lack of investment vehicles. The development of financial services in the city will also need to demand for legal services, accountants, and other consulting services. The infrastructure for this will need a strong regulatory framework.

The final issue is a range of policies to attract high quality human capital: Taxes remain high in the city compared to competitors like Hong Kong. While financial services professionals in Shanghai may feel that they are on high wages, internationally in fact they are relatively low. In this sector in Shanghai, the highest costs are still the renting of buildings, rather than wage costs, as is the case in mature markets. So in this sense, Shanghai is still a very immature market.

But it is a market with huge potential for growth – perhaps more than any other centre in the world. For that reason, the city's positives in financial service for the future outweigh the shorter term challenges it has.

Chapter Seven

Shanghai's Environment

Shanghai's challenges with its environment parallel those which confront the wider condition of China's environment as a whole, and are some of the most urgent and pressing. The solution to them lies at the heart of Shanghai's future. Ideas about the protection of the built and natural environment, during a period when the city is under increasing pressure from rising population levels and greater industrialization, was at the heart of the Expo, particularly in its 'best urban practices area' which showcased ways in which cities throughout the rest of the world were attempting to deal with their needs in the coming decades as resources become scarcer and the impact of man-made climate change is likely to become more intense.

The Five Year Programmes and the various iterations of the city plans outlined in Chapter Two all devote a considerable part of their attention to dealing with aspects of environmental protection. In this chapter, I will look at the issues of Shanghai's sustainability plan, its regeneration efforts, the current and future energy needs of the city, and the preservation of its natural environment along with scenarios for how these extremely important subjects might develop over the coming decade.

China's National Environmental Challenges: Context

Expert on the Chinese environment Judith Shapiro writes in a book on the the country's national challenges:

> 'China's huge environmental challenges are significant for us all. The choices the Chinese Communist Party, national government and local government are making influence not only the health and well-being of China, but also the very future of the planet.'[1]

Through its intense industrialization in the last three decades in particular, China has built up a list of environmental issues, ranging from deforestation and land degradation, to air pollution, and water supply issues. In the last two decades, the country has suffered from a number of extreme weather events, from flooding by the Yangtze River in 1998, to the heavy snowfalls during the Chinese New Year in 2008 which impacted so much on people's travel plans then, and the droughts which the north east of the country in particular has been suffering from since the early 2000s. In 2012, the first paper produced by the State Council that year was on water security. Some estimates state that as much as 75 per cent of the country's rivers and lakes, and 90 per cent of urban groundwater have severe pollution, with 28 per cent of China's rivers ranked category five (the worst), unsuitable even for agricultural use.[2] In the late 2000s, China overtook the US as the world's largest emitter of carbon dioxide. The World Bank from 2005 has assessed that 20 of the world's 30 most polluted cities are in China, much of this due to the energy profile of the country where as much as 75 per cent still comes from fossil fuels, a major cause of carbon emissions.

---

1. Judith Shapiro. *China's Environmental Challenges*. Polity Press, London, 2012, pp.1-2.
2. Ibid., p.8.

Shanghai's Natural Environment

Shanghai's environmental challenges therefore can be contextualized within these very serious national ones. While the issues mentioned above are generic across the country, much of the response has to be local. In that sense, Shanghai's mapping out of strategies to deal with its own environmental issues acts as a case study of what is happening across the country.

Two years before the Expo, the Shanghai International Conference on Development and Environmental Protection was held in the city, in Hongqiao District, in late 2008. Hosted by the then deputy Party Secretary Sha Hailan, the United Nations Environment Programme Director for Asia and the Pacific, and the Director of the Shanghai Environmental Protection Bureau, it went through a number of benchmarks which had been achieved up to then, and looked at the likely future challenges. Since the turn of the decade, up to 3 per cent of annual GDP has been given over to investment in environmental protection and sustainability locally. By 2011, the city invested 55 Billion RMB in environment protection, a figure which had tripled since 2000.

Part of the strategy of the city has been to use a 'Three Convergences' plan. In this, population is concentrated in the towns, industry in industrial parks and agricultural operations increased. Over 2008 to 2011, the objective of becoming an 'environmentally friendly city' has been brought to the fore, largely because it is also critical to delivering the kind of living environment which fulfils the expectations of people already residing in Shanghai but also attracts those from outside. In 2008, Zhang Quan, director of the Shanghai Environment Protection Bureau, stated that the challenge for the city was that 'while maintaining economic growth, it is very important to protect the environment, especially in a city as populated as ours.' He stated that the priority over the coming three years would be the 'promotion of a circular economy and a low carbon economy with noise pollution control being the first priority.' [3]

The key areas in which this was divided were as follows:

- Water: In 2008, Shanghai has 54 sewage treatment plants. Treatment of waste water is a critical issue throughout China, where water supplies have been polluted by intense industrialization, and where the whole process of urbanization has placed enormous strains on the supply of drinking water in cities. A World Bank project earlier in the decade had in particular looked at the water quality of Huangpu River, Suzhou Creek and the Yangtze Estuary, and the success of attempts to clean these up. Up to 2007, 148 monitoring points were put in operation to assess water quality in the municipal area, with 187 major water polluters required to provide online monitoring.

- Air Quality: According to the national Environment Ministry, and the National Development and Reform Commission surveys, air quality is one of the major concerns for Chinese citizens. Its impact on their health is serious, with links to respiratory disease, to skin infections and to general wellbeing. One of the main causes of air pollution in China has been the heavy dependence on fossil fuels to generate energy. Shanghai has partially solved this by moving much heavy industry away from the city as part of the process of its transition towards a service orientated and high-tech economy rather than a heavy manufacturing one. Up to the end of 2008, therefore, nearly 6000 facilities which had used coal before within the inner ring road area where replaced with cleaner energy sources. The city also installed almost 50 automatic ambient air monitoring stations. 70 per cent of inner city pollution comes from cars (see below). Despite all the challenges, air quality has improved in the last decade. In 2000, according to the Shanghai Environmental Protection Bureau, there were 295 days with good ambient air quality a year, with a rate of 80 per cent of

---

3. *China Daily*, 15 December 2008.

days per year with good air quality. By 2011, this has changed to 337 days a year, and 92.3 per cent respectively.

- Waste Treatment: Modernisation and rising living standards in the last three decades has also meant a parallel increase on packaging for food, and the per capita levels of waste produced by each household. In 1978, the city produced 2.4 millions tons of waste, of which half came from residential and half from construction. It also produced 4.18 million tones of night soil. By 2011, these figures had undergone a fascinating change. For waste, the city had increased five fold to 11 million tons per year, with residential producing two thirds of this and construction and industry the remainder. Per capita, however, in view of the rise of population of the city over this period, the increase in waste had doubled rather than risen by a greater proportion. Night soil, however, for a city with a bigger population, has been treated far more efficiently, with the figure halving from its 1978 peak, despite being for more people.

- Transportation: Car usage in Shanghai has continuously risen over the last decade. In 2009, the city had 2.85 million vehicles, of which 1.47 million were passenger vehicles (1.24 million of these being cars), 0.22 million trucks, and 1.28 million motorcycles. By 2011 this had risen to 3.29 million vehicles, of which 1.94 were passenger vehicles (1.63 million of these being cars), 0.24 million trucks and 1.28 million motorbikes. Shanghai is therefore becoming as dependent on car ownership, despite the steep rise in registration and number plate costs over this period. The vast majority of cars were individually owned (over 70 per cent in 2011) rather than company or government ones. In order to offset this, construction of mass transport from metro lines to light railway and buses have all received significant investment. In 2000, the city had 257 kilometres of railways and 5970 kilometres of highways. With its 13 metro lines to the end of 2012, and 292 stations, Shanghai now has 434 kilometres of rail, making it the third longest in the world after Seoul and Beijing. In 2011, it carried 2.1 billion people, with a record daily usage of 7.4 million passengers on October 22nd 2010.

- Climate Change: Shanghai is a port. Rising sea levels will have an immense impact on the city if they happen. For that reason, support for measures against climate change is critical. In 2000, Shanghai set itself a goal of reducing energy consumption per unit of GDP by 20 per cent by 2009. Part of the plan for this was to produce more of its energy by wind, solar, biomass and renewables. A critical objective here is diversifying and changing the city's energy profile away from fossil fuels.

Shanghai Energy

Since 1990, Shanghai's energy needs have increased dramatically. In 1990, it used 319 million tones Standard Coal Equivalent (SCE), of which over 75 per cent was used by industry. But in 2011, this had risen to 1.12 billion tons SCE, with a little over a half going to industry. The growth rate over this period saw rises in every year, with particular steep rises in the mid 2000s.

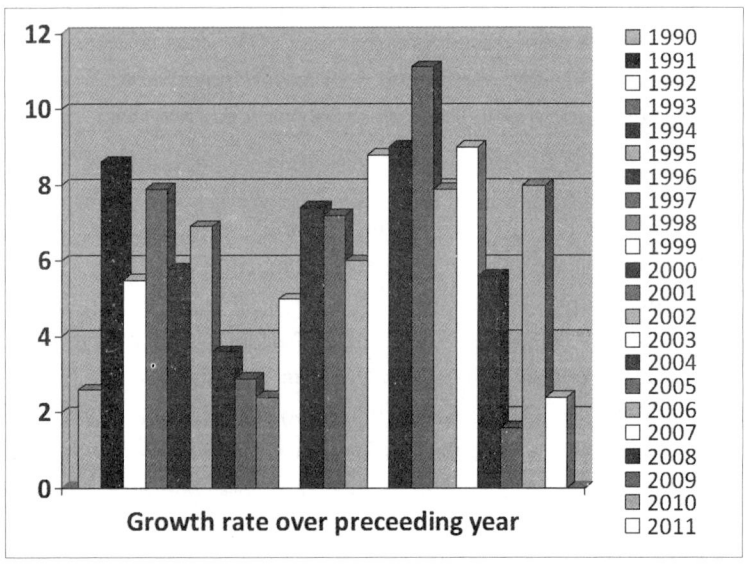

Growth rate over preceeding year

From 2008, as with the rest of the country, the main source of energy was coal (a half of the total energy consumed in 2011), and the main user industry.

In terms of carbon emissions, the city has been at the forefront of trying to tackle these, with a carbon trade platform launched in August 2012, aimed at making companies with large carbon footprints pay for their emissions. According to a report in the China Daily, this will involve 200 companies across 16 industries, particularly those in steel, petrochemicals, non-ferrous metals and power. It will be based in the Shanghai Environment and Energy Exchange. [4]

The Regeneration of the City

Shanghai is a city with over a century and a half of history as a modern commercial century, and many centuries before this as a place where people lived and worked. This has given it a rich architectural inheritance, part of which was looked at in the descriptions of the Bund in Chapter One. The history of the various phases of the city's development is remembered in its streets and in the built legacy that has been left behind.

Many of these buildings are no longer usable for the purposes for which they were originally built. Here the city shares a common challenge with others that went through previous phases of industrialization and then need to create appropriate urban spaces by which to undertake new economic functions. Warehouses, port

---

4. *China Daily*, 27 July 2012.

buildings, and factories have changed radically. The port has moved many of its functions away from the original location. Warehouses have grown vast, and are outside the main urban living areas. Factories are mostly now placed in special industrial zones. Processes have changed from even two decades ago, as have work philosophies.

Caring for Shanghai's historic built legacy is important for many reasons. Firstly, it creates a sense of historic continuity, physically representing some of the inheritance from the past to people who are now living there. This is important for the creation of a sense of unique and local Shanghai identity. Secondly, many of the industrial and commercial buildings in Shanghai are of importance as remnants of former phases of innovation, with some of the world's earliest concrete or steel structure buildings. Thirdly, many of these buildings are important for tourism and for the increasingly significant heritage industry, something which the rising numbers of tourists coming to Shanghai testify to. Finally, the maintenance of these historic sites is important for the sustainability agenda, with significant benefits both for the environment and economically in their preservation.

Even so, a comprehensive preservation programme is not straightforward. Not least of the challenges is making sure that older buildings are renovated to modern standards and don't become stagnant islands adrift in an economy which is fast moving away from them. Land is at a premium in the city, with so many new residents moving in. Every building has to justify its existence in this highly competitive environment. The experience of regeneration over the last two decades has given the city much knowledge about what works. Perhaps the most symbolic site has been Xintiandi, a development in the middle of where the old French Concession was, and a place which has been radically transformed in the last decade.

The person at the heart of this was Vincent Lo, a native of Hong Kong but with family links to Shanghai, who had been coming on business to the city since the mid 1980s when he had worked with the Communist Youth League (see below). Lo's involvement with

Xintiandi started in 1997 when the Shui On Group of which he is Chair, first raised the idea of redeveloping this residential area which is located close to the site where the building which housed the opening days of the First Congress of the Communist Party in 1921 is located. The project broke ground in 1999, and the first phase, at a cost of USD150 million, was completed in late 2001. In 2012, it constitutes a space of 30 thousand square metres, with restaurants, shops, and residential buildings. Phase three of the redevelopment was opened in 2010. The chief architect of the development, American Ben Wood, was someone who had not worked in China before becoming involved in the project at Vincent Lo's introduction in the early 2000s. Wood has stated that his objective has not been so much to preserve as to redefine places. 'The real point,' he stated in a newspaper interview in 2006, 'is not the architecture of the place, but the new life a place attracts. The hutong probably should be torn down. They can't even accommodate sewage pipes, let alone cables for everything else people need today. That doesn't mean destroy the kind of places they are.' [5]

The Redevelopment of Xintiandi

Vincent Lo, Chair of Shui On Group, felt from the time he had been living in the city in the late 1980s that it would become an increasingly important finance and commercial centre, even though at that time it had not even been accorded Special Economic Zone status. Asked by then Mayor Xu Kuangdi to nurture links between Hong Kong and Shanghai, he was building on strong historic ties which had seen many people move between the cities over the preceding century. Lo asked

---

5. Julie V. Iovine. 'Our Man in Shanghai: Ben Wood Takes on History'. *New York Times*, 13 August 2006.

international experts to do a master plan of how they might envisage redeveloping the Xintiandi first phase in the late 1990s. One of the most appealing aspects was to try to create more green spaces with a more open, natural feel. This was behind the construction of a lake in the district which cost almost 1 billion RMB, part funded by the city government and part by Shui On.

There were, of course, setbacks. When the project was first discussed in 1997, the property market as a result of hyper inflation in the city was poor. What gave the project impetus a little later were two important symbolic events – the 80th anniversary of the founding of the Communist Party of China in 2001, and the Asia Pacific Economic Cooperation (APEC) meeting, due to be held in the city in October that year.

The redevelopment of a high profile site like Xintiandi was a good way of maximizing the public exposure from these two events. But one of the main challenges was to negotiate packages for the 3500 families who lived in the area to find housing elsewhere so that the redevelopment, once approved, could actually begin. One of the impacts of this was to make clear that Xintiandi would only work as a mixed residential and commercial centre.

A further challenge was in terms of finance. Building the area needed bank support, but local banks who were a natural source of loans had little understanding for the reasons behind the project and why it might become commercially viable. Finding an architect who was sympathetic to the aims of the project was also important. This eventually led to the appointment of American architect Ben Wood (see above) who has maintained a link to the project to this day. Vincent Lo decided thirty minutes after meeting Wood that he was the right person for the work.

As a sign of how much new work is involved in regenerating older locations, 80 per cent of the physical infrastructure of Xintiandi had to be rebuilt, albeit using recycled old materials. The main philosophy was to try to achieve use of the past to speak about the future, and show that there was a connection between the lifestyle aspirations of people who had lived a century before in totally different cultural and economic circumstances, and those of today. Xintiandi was above all designed to attempt to create a sense of community.

As a result of the experiences from XIntiandi's redevelopment, Shui On Land limited is now developing a more purely residential area, Rainbow City, in Hongkou district, which aims to have 10 high rise residential buildings with a floor space of 1.5 million square metres over the next few years.

■■■■■■■■■■■■■■■■■■■■■■

Regeneration projects inspired by the success of Xintiandi and the early redevelopments of specific buildings have now increased. Connected with the Shanghai Expo in 2010, there was the Bund Redevelopment Project, which was managed by US firm Chan Krieger Sieniewicz. The redevelopment of the Promenade in particular involved digging three kilometers of tunnel underneath to accommodate traffic, at a cost of USD586 million, and which took three years. Associated with this has been the subsequent Rockbund complex development, incorporating four acres to the north of the Bund which are being developed under the Rockefeller Group.

The New Built Environment

Over the last three decades, Shanghai has seen the construction of over two thousand sky scrapers. Where once the tallest buildings in the city were along the Bund, the Pudong area opposite now has three of the world's highest structures. The physical nature of the city has changed dramatically and quickly. But this explosion of buildings has created its own set of challenges. One of them is the issue of land stability. Much of Shanghai is on marsh, land which needs to be reinforced and strengthened to build such vast structures. In Edward Dennison and Guang Yu Ren's book on Shanghai, they refer to the real challenges of trying to create a city where the buildings are now becoming heavier and bigger, and the pressure on resources and on the land greater.[6]

The other issue is the amount of energy that buildings use. They account for about 50 per cent of energy usage, through heating, air conditioning and their maintenance. Their energy efficiency is therefore very critical. Shanghai has seen a number of experiments in trying to make buildings carbon neutral. More are being powered by renewable sources of energy. Greater effort has gone into making sure that they are efficient, well insulated, and even that they have greenery and other natural materials to help in their efficiency. This obviously adds to the initial costs of building, although in the long term, of course, it delivers sounder economic returns.

The creation of a mega city, which is what, in effect, Shanghai is becoming, leads to discussion about mixed use zones, where hotels, entertainment, museums, public offices, businesses and residential accommodation are all located. The city has some of the most innovative new architecture, but it is also struggling with areas which are in danger of becoming deprived, or left behind, such as Nanshi District (now one part under the jurisdiction of Huangpu District), which has lower economic and social development indicators than other parts of the city. Buildings in these areas can quickly become run down and symbolize inequality and alienation. The need for green spaces and public areas is important, to assist in creating the

---

6. Edward Denison; Guang Yu Ren. *Building Shanghai: The Story of China's Gateway*. Wiley Academy, Singapore, 2006

sense of cohesion in a highly mobile, dynamic and ever changing city – one that personifies the concept of 'liquid modernity.' Public spaces in which people interact and feel secure are a critical part of the living infrastructure of cities, and counterbalance the private and business spaces.

In the coming decade, with the pressure on land and the rise in population, the city will see more sky scrapers, and the need for deeper experimentation in how to build efficient, mixed use structures. According to one long term resident in the city, Shanghai is now at the cutting edge of constructing buildings over 60 floors, simply though the number that are built each year. This skill will become more useful for other cities in China going through similar redevelopments, and for those elsewhere in the developing world. It will also be of importance to cities in the developed world which are looking to regenerate.

Food Security

While there is much discussion of energy, resource and even water security, discussion of food security often gets neglected. This might seem strange to apply to a city-level entity, rather than talking in national terms. Even so, Shanghai is at the forefront of a consumer, and a diet revolution, as seen in previous chapters in this book. And its issues over food security are symptomatic of those which are ongoing across the whole of China.

Nationally, since 1978 China has been able to feed a fifth of the world's population with only 7 per cent of the world's arable land. Through a combination of new technology, new fertilizers, and new strains of cereals and stable crops it has been able to produce bumper harvests in the late 2000s. Even so, the country has 120 million people who are living below the nationally agreed poverty line, and as many as 24 million who are defined as malnourished. It is also facing a revolution in eating habits, with more meat replacing vegetables and vegetarian dishes. This is placing new pressures on the food supply chain. In particular, China has become a major importer of soya in recent years, which is used in the production of beef. It has also started to import corn. In 2010, the country has a USD200 million deficit in food stuffs, becoming a new importer after many years of self sufficiency.[7]

Shanghai symbolizes many of these changes. It has seen intense urbanization, with agricultural land increasingly turned over for industrial and commercial or residential use. Pudong typifies this, a place where there were farms into recently, but which is now almost wholly taken up by commercial buildings and non-agricultural land use. While the city still has some food growing areas, and a surprising amount of rural land within the municipal border, it is reliant for almost all its food on imports, either from other areas of China, or from abroad. According to the Shanghai Department of Commerce, in interviews in November 2012, there are 129 farms across the country exclusively sending food to Shanghai, with huge cooperation deals with farms in the north eastern province of Heilongjiang. This has gone some way to creating a competitive internal market from which to supply the city's food needs. Even so, the issue of feeding a city which is growing in number of people so rapidly and where there are rising demands for luxury foods or energy intensive foods is a serious one.

---

7. I am grateful to Professor Robert Ash for some of the information in this section.

Sustainability and the Environment: The Bigger Picture

In her book on China's environmental challenges, American expert Judith Shapiro sets out five core concepts linked to sustainability which help to understand it and the policy impact of choices made in this area better. These are:

- The implications of globalization
- Challenges of governance
- Issues of national identity
- Civil society
- Environmental justice [8]

She talks of these in a national context, but in fact they can help to understand Shanghai's position and its choices in the next decade as it attempts to become a sustainable city, with greater energy efficiency, and a stronger sense of food and resource security.

In terms of globalization, there are few areas where it is less easy to draw neat geographical boundaries around issues than the environment or resources. In terms of the food it needs, its water, and the quality of its air, Shanghai has very limited powers on its own to control these. It has to devise truly global solutions in partnership inside and outside China, and to fundamentally globalise its thinking and its conceptual framework. Just as it will need in the future to radically open its doors to international capital flows and to migration flows in the coming decade, to continue being at the forefront of Chinese globalization, so will it also have to practice this 'global mindset; in how it handles its environmental challenges. The city will both be a leader in innovation for places elsewhere in the

---

8. Judith Shapiro. op. cit., pp.11-12.

world in terms of how it builds efficient buildings, but also learning how to create a balanced, multi zoned city where it avoids deep inequalities across communities. In terms of ideas, too, as Shapiro points out, 'while the flow of goods and capital provides much of the impetus for China's environmental problems, the flow of people and ideas provides mitigating possibilities.'[9] This shows itself in the ways in which China participates in international discussions and fora on climate change, and how its intellectual communities participate in discussions and activities on the global response to environmental and resource problems.

For governance, it is clear that a regulatory framework and strong implementation strategies will continue to be key to addressing environmental problems. A legal framework with the right enforcement needs to be in place, arrived at after consultation and discussion. This happens at local, national and global level. For Shanghai, the challenge is to balance the needs of an increasingly better educated, and demanding population with pragmatic growth objectives. Public participation in decision making, the formulation of well articulated rules and the right enforcement mechanisms are all part of this. Without strong governance, solving environmental challenges will almost be impossible, because they will involve clear policy choices and strict implementation strategies that are accepted across society as fair and necessary, even though at times they may well involve sacrifice or unexpected change. In this process, there will be winners and losers, and socially negotiated settlements in which all sides need to make compromises. The moral and intellectual authority of those managing and governing this process will be critical. Here Shanghai, at the forefront of the Chinese economy, can also be at the forefront of its experiments in public participation, amongst a well informed population. Management of the environment will be an area in which all should, and must feel they are stakeholders.

National Identity is the most complex. Each citizen carries multi

---

9. Judith Shapiro. op. cit., p.17.

identities, whether they be religious, cultural, provincial, tribal. One can be human, Asian, Chinese and Shanghainese. Even within Shanghainese, one can be native born, or from outside. How these identities are internalized and linked to specific places and feelings about those places is important. For a highly dynamic, mobile city, the sense of how people feel they belong to Shanghai even if they are newly moved to the city, and what sort of stakeholder they are in the development and the environment of the city are important. As an emerging, developing country, China and its people have a distinctive feeling about their economic growth and how it relates to their status in the world, and also about how others from outside China can speak to them about what they need or should do to address environmental challenges. Part of this is the debate about what specific vision for modernity and development China has. In adopting some of the aspects of industrialization and consumption from North America, Europe and other capitalist societies, China has had to balance its specific view of its own indigenous needs and development with the attractions of what other systems offer. But it has also had to wrestle with the huge issues of sustainability that this has brought. In many ways, the Chinese process of modernity will need to involve radical new ideas about consumption and sustainability. Shanghai is likely to be the first place because of its advanced per capita income levels and the nature of its economy to see what the national vision of development and modernity look like. As Shapiro argues, 'the preoccupation with reasserting China's rightful place of respect in the world underlies many of China's developmental decisions and helps us understand the important role of national identity in China's prospects for achieving sustainable development.'[10]

As a corollary of governance, civil society is the fourth key issue. In the coming decade, the growth of civil society in China will prove critical in addressing issues of social cohesion (see Chapter Two) but also building broad social alliances to work on the governance

---

10. Judith Shapiro. op. cit., p.20.

issues mentioned above. The role of consent, of social negotiation in order to decide on a course of action and then implement it, will grow stronger as society becomes more complex. Civil society and its growth in the last three decades in China has been remarkable. Shanghai, like many other regions of China, has seen the multiplication of groups focusing on the environment, on protection of civic heritage, and on the protection of nature. These groups will be key partners for various levels of government in the coming decade as a broader social effort is made to tackle the modes of human behavior that lead to waste and climate change. The supervision of civil society groups through a stronger enabling legal infrastructure, and support for ways in which they can represent different kinds of public opinion in Shanghai, will be important. In this area, environmental groups can perform an enormously important social function and contribute both to cohesion and governance, in giving voice to sectors of society so that they feel they are participating and are part of the development of the city as a whole.

Finally, there is environmental justice. This involves the understanding and discussion of the broad rights of any one or any group to use resources which are often fiercely competed for. Shapiro refers to the concept of 'shadow ecology.' When we calculate the 'carbon footprint' for an individual, an organization or even a country, we have to ask a number of questions. 'From where does it extract the resources it consumes? To where does it export its waste? What are the hidden costs of daily choices?' [11] Placing environmentally damaging manufacturing plants outside the city only displaces their impact, it doesn't remove it. In that sense, as a consumption centre Shanghai now answers to the same kinds of questions that developed countries get who receive manufactured goods from developing countries. They are simply outsourcing problematic carbon emissions and waste material, but not dealing with the fundamental issue. In that sense, Shanghai has a major role to play domestically in addressing the national challenges, and by sharing best practice and new techniques.

---

11. Judith Shapiro. op. cit., p.22.

These five areas therefore provide themes within which the very specific and practical challenges of the environment and sustainability can be better analysed, understood and thereby addressed. They also help to explain why the specific role that Shanghai plays in the national economy means that it is central in each of these areas in to the national debate, and will continue to be important in the formulation of solutions both to China's needs in this area, but also in ways which have international relevance. What Shanghai does in the next decade in these areas will not just be of local significance, but of global importance, in showing where the country is heading and what ways it will deal with its challenges in an area that is critical to humanity.

Chapter Eight

Shanghai Culture

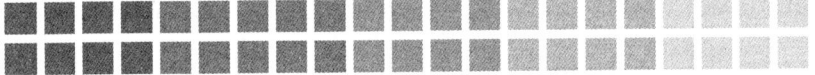

The novels of Qiu Xiaolong have received international acclaim. His inspector Chen has to investigate some of the murkiest cases that happen in the city, involving murder, theft and abduction. In one of the most popular, 'Death of A Red Heroine', a former national model worker is found dead in a canal. Chen's investigation of the death leads him into many secret paths and hidden away corners of the city. But there are many ways in which the city itself, written about so atmospherically by Qiu who is a native of Shanghai and was born there in 1953, is the real star of the book. A description of Chen's residence in the early part of the book goes:

> *'It was a sweltering Friday afternoon. Occasionally cicadas could be heard chirping on a poplar tree outside the window of his new one bedroom apartment on the second floor of a gray brick building. From the window, he could look out over busy traffic moving slowly along Huaihai Road, but at a desirable, noiseless distance. The building was conveniently located near the centre of Luwan District. It took him less that twenty minutes to walk to Nanking Road in the north, or to the City God's Temple in the south, and on a clear summer night, he could smell the tangy breeze from the Huangpu River.'* [1]

---

1. Qiu Xiaolong. *Death of a Red Heroine*. Soho Crime, New York, 2000.

Qiu moved to the US in 1988, in order to write a book about T S Eliot, and remains based there at St Louis, Missouri, to this day. He has written seven Inspector Chen stories so far, all set in Shanghai, and all immensely successful. One of the characteristics of his writing is the loving descriptions of food and eating which his books contain.

Shanghai's literary heritage is important, and contributes to the sense of the city as a cultural centre. Perhaps the most famous writer to be based in the city in modern times was the great Lu Xun, who made Shanghai his home after a peripatetic existence from 1927, dying there a decade later in 1936. Lu Xun however was only one of a group of left wing writers, all of whom were active when the city was also a major film and theatre centre.

Shanghai today attracts world class performers, ranging from the Vienna Philharmonic Orchestra to the Rolling Stones. It has three major venues in the Shanghai Concert Hall, home to the symphony orchestra based in the city, the Grand Theatre, and the Oriental Art Centre. It also has a plethora of galleries, museums and other performance places.

The issue has recurred throughout this book that in order to fulfill the ambition to be a global and globalizing city, but one with a strong sense of its own identity, Shanghai needs both the soft and hard infrastructure for culture. The Expo of 2010 was a means of trying to convey some of this cultural ambition, allowing a number of visiting performance artists to come from across the world. The city has supported an increasingly vibrant modern art biannual exhibition, and has created a modern art museum next to the older one by the Municipal City Hall. Cultural development, however, is one of the most vexed issues to try to define, and one of the hardest to be prescriptive about. Shanghai has great assets, and in its heritage inspirational moments of creativity. In order to be a mega-city, and to have the diversity and scope of a modern metropolis which attracts people from across the world, culture will be critical. But how precisely it does this is not a simple question.

The city plans contain ideas about fulfilling these cultural aspirations, with supportive language. The 12th Five Year Programme for the city talks of building a 'cultural city', with an admission that there is a life beyond producing GDP growth, however important this is, and creating lifestyles and new narratives for people to live in and find fulfillment and value. Soft power (see below) is critical to this. The Programme refers to building what it calls 'cultural and civilization infrastructure', reinforced through the preservation of old buildings, and the opening of a great international cultural communication centre. Tourism has become a major economic sector for the new service orientated economy that is being created, and for that too cultural attractions are important.

Culture relates closely to the issues which were discussed in the chapter on environment. It impacts on globalization, on issues of identity, on civil society and on values. Shanghai is a place which has undergone radical change in the last decades. In a very short period of time it has physically, socially and economically transformed. It is now the home to a complex and highly mobile population, and one with a wide range of different values and identities. It is not surprising therefore that the issue of the city's overall identity, its brand as it were, is so important. That links both to the places it has been before, and its historic identity, but also to the things it now is, and the places it wishes to become.

Soft Power

The term coined by American diplomat and intellectual Joseph Nye of a nation's soft power assets has become embedded in much Chinese government and administrative discourse. Chinese soft power nationally has been intensely studied, both through the creation of Confucian Institutes and also through the holding of major events like the Beijing Olympics and the Shanghai Expo. Nye originally defined soft power in a world where, in 1991, 'power is becoming less fungible, less coercive, and less tangible... Co-optive behavioural power – getting others to want what you want – and soft power resources – cultural attractions, ideology, and international institutions – are not new.... Yet various trends are making co-optive behavior and sort power resources more important.'[2] He went on, 'soft power rests on the ability to shape the preferences of others' because other countries admire its values, and wish to be like it. Specifically about China, however, Nye, while recognizing the immense soft power assets that the country could have, also saw the challenges: 'The real promise for China and India still lies in the future,' he stated.

There are ways in which Shanghai exemplifies how Chinese soft power might look in the coming decade. We can group these into several discrete areas:

- Shanghai as a centre for Chinese visions of internationalization and modernity: The city has been built on a number of previous phases of international business, movement of people, and flow of ideas. Its openness, both to the world, to the region and to the rest of China — the place, as one commentator said, where East meets West, and where East also meets East – are tangibly symbolized in the ways in which the city embraces modern forms of architecture, ideas about city planning, ideas about how to live life in a modern mixed and dynamic economy, and how to be open to the outside world while maintaining one's own values and identity. Shanghai's logistic and commercial openness are all facilitators of this, and mean that in terms of capital flows, of embracing new ideas about how to do business, and about how to integrate this, the city is at the forefront of internationalization in China. It therefore carries immense soft power through its open embrace of internationalization, and what this means in practice in a Chinese context.

---

2. Mauro F. Guillen; Emilio Ontiveros. op. cit., pp.134–135.

- Shanghai as a place of diversity: In order to find highly skilled, well educated and global workers, Shanghai will need to continue being a place that attracts outsiders to come and settle. These come both from within China and across the world. The concept of 'being Shanghainese' therefore will need to be a very flexible one. It will be a group that diverse constituents can join, and will have to have an openness and non-exclusivity in order to embrace the large number of people who will continue to come to the city. A diverse sense of identity that can accommodate people's different ethnicities, life styles, and beliefs, will be critically important if social tension and conflict are to be avoided between groups. The city being a place of tolerance, where people can fulfill their ambitions but in ways that do not impede and cause strife with others will be important. The pressures on the physical environment and the living space in the city will only increase as its population rises. Modes of governance and public communication will be important in order to prevent conflict between different officials and people. The city will have an image of diversity which will help contradict the stereotyped ideas of uniformity and collectiveness which are sometimes still held outside of China about the country.

- Shanghai as a place of individuality: With dynamic and new identities, people in Shanghai can have the social space and the tolerance around them to be able to articulate their interests, and their core values in ways which fulfill themselves, but also avoid impeding on others who wish to live different lifestyles. Shanghai as a middle class, service orientated, consumption led economy will allow us to see new types of personal liberty amongst young Chinese, but also new forms of responsibility and participation in civic and public life. Shanghai will be a place therefore where we will increasingly see the interface between social held ambitions to create together a rich, strong and successful modernizing economy, alongside the space for people to create their own personal lives, make their own choices and articulate their own life goals.

- Shanghai as a networked city: Shanghai will typify the new society evolving across China, and in the developed world – a world where individuals are able to create supporting business, personal and cultural networks around themselves through social media and through the creation linkages, friendships, and intimacies which are enabling but also challenge notions of what society actually is in the 21st century. The ways in which Shanghainese are able to develop a sense of their society as a whole, as somewhere they can belong to and find value in, but also how they can empower themselves through the creation of a networked space around them as individuals will be one of the key issues in the coming decade. The challenge of managing networks but not being overwhelmed by them will be intense in the city, as will addressing the issues of meaning and observing respect for people and their personal space that the Internet has aroused elsewhere.

In a city of such dynamic change, in which almost daily things are changing, and where everything is in flux, the issue of belonging and of cultural traction is an important one, both for individuals but also for policy makers. In the end, society can only ever be a collection of people, with their different life histories, their inherited and learned behavioural traits, their aspirations, hopes and dreams. Their lives in the rich tapestry of the city are dependent on their own resilience, creativity and energy, but also on the environment around them and what it provides them in terms of inspiration, material well being, support and opportunity.

People within this city context can create meaning through the ways in which they identify themselves. And that might depend on their ethnicity, their family, their religious or political beliefs – a raft of complex ingredients that make people what they are. Shanghai in many ways utterly symbolizes the liquidity of modern Chinese life – the liquidity and mobility of goods, of people, of ideas, of capital. This mobility has been immensely liberating. It means that people can seek new opportunities and try to create new ways to live which better suit their inner aspirations. But it can also be challenging, alienating, and disorientating. Cynicism, a lack of value, a feeling of placelessness and not belonging are all well understood, well described but hard to cure side effects of rapid modernization.

The Culture of a City of Wellbeing

One great challenge is to shift from focusing on tangible and easily measured outcomes of productivity, like GDP growth, to looking at other ways to trying to define what successful living in a modern city like Shanghai with its complexity and diversity and energy might mean. Wellbeing in terms of health is one, although the life expectancy and the physical health of people has improved greatly in the last three decades. Deeper than this is the issue of meaning, of how people find value in their lives, of how they give free expression to their creativity, and how they are able to hope and dream.

Social media has been a way of having insight into the inner lives of many modern Chinese, although it is still an area about which the rest of the world is often puzzled. Are Chinese believers solely in family, in society, in the greatness of their country, in their destiny to become a modern major power, or in the wealth and the benefits this has brought them in recent years? What do they want from society, and what sort of society and life are they aiming for as they become richer? On Chinese social media, there are often expressions of cynicism, hopelessness, and feeling of disorientating arising from the many changes that have happened in the past three decades. On the other hand, there are also many expressions of dynamism, hope, and wonder at the new possibilities that have been opened up. There are no simple or uniform dominant voices within this new society. This therefore offers a great challenge to create a cultural framework which manages to embrace all of this, in ways which enhances people's sense of being valued and doing things that are of value, but also allows them to feel in control of their lives and part of the greater society they are located in.

Identity through creating a brand or a message about what the city is is important. Any branding is a complex process, trying to link the emotions that a product or a place arouses with some basis in what needs it supplies, and what it appeals to. For Shanghai, the key challenge for soft power promotion is to somehow gather up all the aspirations, the dynamism, the traditions and the heritage as a place of globalization and openness but one which is distinctly Chinese and convey them in something powerful and recognizable to those inside and outside China. Branding Shanghai will be a major challenge, but one which will be critical for its meaning as a city to its own inhabitants and also to the outside world.

What Does It Mean to Be Shanghainese?

What in fact does it mean, in the first part of the 21st century, to say that you are Shanghainese? This was the kind of question others asked of themselves during periods when other cities expanded rapidly, taking in an influx of new people. What does it mean to be a Londoner, a Parisian, or a New Yorker? How do people internalize the values of the city they have moved to, and how to they come to feel they 'belong'? The city of London in the UK has 50 per cent of its current population born out of the country. New York is similarly cosmopolitan. For Shanghai, while the international component might not be as high, in terms of those born and raised outside the city in other parts of China, the figure might be even higher. Native born Shanghainese are a minority now, and proportionally are only likely to grow smaller.

For those who have come to the city, what are the core feelings that they adopt in order to be able to feel that they are also native – that they have become local? Shanghai has its own foodstyle, its own dialect, its own history and customs. But beyond trying to adopt these, what accommodations within oneself does one have to make to become Shanghainese, and perhaps more importantly, what rewards and benefits does one get in adopting this new place? And how extensive can this be? Can a European or an Australian eventually also feel like they have become Shanghainese? Surely in a global city, this should now be possible.

As Shanghai evolves and develops, it will be at the forefront of trying to answer some of these questions. We will live in an era in which (as the concluding chapter will show) the tension between our identity as national inhabitants and global citizens will only grow more intense. The processes of globalization are deepening and growing wider. In that sense, many Shanghainese will wrestle with one local form of a problem which is generic across the planet: How can I feel I belong here when I am from elsewhere.

Many people will locate the true meaning of this question in terms of where they have come from, their past experiences, and their former happinesses. In that sense, there will always be a slight nostalgia, or a feeling of a golden age in the past that people are fond of looking back to. But one of the attractions of the future, as opposed to the past, is that anything still can happen. Shanghai is a place which, as many who have been interviewed during the research for this book made clear, doesn't just work with its heritage in order to create an identity and a culture, but also to build a future. It is a place where the future seems to be arriving quicker than elsewhere, with all the liberating energy but also anxiety and lack of certainty that brings.

Cultural Innovation

Previous chapters have talked of the importance of innovation. This applies to the economy, to industrial processes and the making of new products. But there are multiple forms of innovation, and many different ways to innovate. Shanghai is becoming a city that should encourage and nurture cultural innovation, using its enormous human and natural assets, and the many different kinds of experience that people are having in the city. Cultural infrastructure includes theatres, cinemas, concert halls, all of which are being built, and the organizations and funding around orchestras, acting groups, writing groups, and libraries, etc. But it also includes the far harder assets of an open environment, and one that enables people's creativity, and helps them feel that they are living a fulfilling life.

Shanghai culture can often appear highly materialistic. Issues of how people deal with newly found wealth occur across societies. One challenge within the city is to create a sense of social belonging and a willingness by citizens to donate their time, their effort and their talents to the larger society, in order to assist in building social cohesion. Citizens become actors and willing agents in this process rather than act passively within it. Most importantly, the philanthropy that has developed in other societies needs to grow stronger in Shanghai. Many of the wealthy do donate to social causes, and there is growing interest in supporting arts groups, and in activity in the cultural realm. This is something that needs to grow in the years ahead.

Cultural innovation also involves spaces where people can take risks with their creativity, where there is tolerance for the ways other people express themselves, and where there is a sense of zones within the city space where communities who have interests in specific kinds of creativity can collect and share what they have. The creation of these networks with social media is now much easier – and Shanghai is home to multiple small groups of like-minded creative figures. Organic growth of these zones without government support is natural. The main thing is to allow the space for this to happen, rather than actively setting up systems and procedures.

The Shanghai Brand

Culture will also be a major part of the Shanghai brand – the branding of a new city which represents Chinese visions of modernity. The debate about modernity in China has existed for over a hundred years, from when in the late Qing Dynasty the promoters of the minor reforms then , like Kang Youwei and Liang Qichao, used their experience of exposure to new ideas from abroad to articulate a local sense of the modern. The May Fourth Movement with the call to follow Mr Science and Mr Democracy in 1919 after the unfair settlement at the end of the First World War typified this. The view that Chinese intellectuals had of modernity in this period was of societies in Europe and North America industrializing, urbanizing, and undergoing radical social and political change, and that this was something China wished to embrace. The cultural impact was also profoundly attractive, expressed through education, the access to books and the creation of films and other modes of mass communication.

Many facets of this industrialization were introduced into China, particularly in Shanghai where the majority of the early factories and modern companies were established. But China remained an agrarian society, even after 1949, and its challenges in overcoming the weight of tradition, of old technology, and of old ways of doing things was not so easy to shift. What was uppermost in the minds of many from 1978 was how to adapt the processes of deeper industrialization and technical innovation and change that had now occurred in Japan, South Korea and other formerly agrarian economies and to create a specifically Chinese form of modernity from this.

The construction of Chinese modernity continues to this day. In much of the rebuilding of Shanghai and its protection and regeneration of its heritage, however, we see complex currents and countercurrents of different forces and traditions. Shanghai's physical environment contains buildings from previous eras of globalization, but also places and gardens which typify former expressions of national identity. Temples have been rebuilt, linking into religious traditions that have long existed, and continue to exist in the city. Museums contain artifacts going back to the earliest dynasties evidencing continuities with previous cultural traditions. Being Chinese is now, in Shanghai, being Modern Chinese in Shanghai in the 21st Century during a period of late modernity and globalization. The main questions for the city therefore are how to express this sense of being both Chinese, with all that that might mean, with also being modern and evolving and developing.

For the city brand therefore, there are three elements to capture:

- The dynamism, energy and optimism of Shanghai. The sense of a city that is full of possibilities and which is looking towards the future, to a world which is better, more equal, and more sustainable.

- Combining elements of what it means to be Chinese and what it is to be international – how can one be committed and belong to a specific place and have a sense of linkage there, but also be global in terms of outlook and ideas.

- The values of Shanghainese – articulating ideas about equal opportunity, about optimism and energy, and about balance and sustainability which are attractive to those outside and help them define and understand the city.

Branding Shanghai is a major challenge. Taking its many different identities, and its complex and rich history, and making them into one powerful image or sentiment is hard. City branding in other countries has taken a while to get right. New York is the big apple. London defines itself as 'the world in one city.' Kuala Lumpa used the phrase 'truly Asian.' Lifestyle and life values are also involved. Sydney promotes its clean environment, its beautiful natural harbor and the outdoors life in its city branding. For San Francisco, the water front and the diversity and tolerance of the city environment are all important, along with its creativity. Branding Shanghai will be a major component of how the city faces a world which will increasingly see it as exemplifying processes of modernization and of a world in which China as a country will increasingly play a major role.

Conclusion

Shanghai 2020

Conceptual frameworks are important. One of the people interviewed for this work said that Shanghai alone had the conceptual framework in China for an international finance centre. In the chapter on the environment too, the conclusion was that Shanghai needed to embrace a conceptual framework that included issues of identity, justice, globalization, governance and civil society in order to manage its challenges in the coming decades. In this final chapter, I will look on three levels at what sort of conceptual frameworks might help in fulfilling Shanghai's objectives of becoming a global, balanced, prosperous and sustainable city by 2020. These frameworks, provided by works by the World Bank and by two analysts based in Europe and the US, will work on the local, national and global level. In each of these areas, we will see that Shanghai has specific experiences that it can offer to the generic global processes of urbanization, social cohesion and the creation of mega cities and the role of emerging economies and the lifestyles that citizens in those places wish to live in the coming decades. Shanghai's future story will, therefore, be intimately linked to the future of the country, the region and the rest of the world. The following is based on this fundamental statement.

The Local Dimension

Yusuf and Nabeshima's World Bank comparative study of Shanghai and Beijing issued in 2010 contains the following six proposals for the city's future development. These are, as they make clear 'a partial redirection of Shanghai's redevelopment strategy', and offer an introduction to 'better recipes' rather than engaging in more cooking. These six proposals are:

• Emphasis on a balanced development of manufacturing and services to maintain the share of manufacturing in municipal output in the 25 per cent to 30 per cent range over the longer term. Their argument is that an overreliance on the financial services sector for growth is unrealistic, and that manufacturing will continue to be an important producer for GDP in the city, even though the sectors in which manufacturing occurs will differ from the past. The key objective is to create a mixed economy in Shanghai, in order to have job creation, and to utilize the full human and natural assets of the city.

• Prioritise activities with reference to longer term profitability, local links and value added as well as cope for innovation and export prospects. In particular, the support for manufacturing of specialist high technology equipment which delivers value added and demands highly skilled and educated labour to produce, and which can drive the city's innovation strategy.

• To concentrate on process innovation by leading firms rather than product innovation. Process innovation is often overlooked in discussions of innovation generally, but it plays an important part in delivering efficiency, and the accession of new ideas. Process also involves the ways in which new management techniques can be brought in and human capital deployed in new ways. For this strategy to work, there needs to be space in the city for a balance between small companies which are usually willing to take risks in the ways in which they operate and to be more flexible about their work methods, and larger firms which are often the first to be able to utilize the new techniques in ways which can commercialise more deeply what small firms have discovered.

• Promote tertiary education and health care, and cultivate strong links between these and other industries. Healthcare is likely to be a major growth sector in Shanghai, with an ageing, longer living population and one which is increasingly prosperous and has higher expectations towards health care. Healthcare is also a major utiliser of highly trained educated talent and a key area of innovation which takes careful long term investment. The development of a pharmaceutical sector in Shanghai through relationships with the research capacity of universities will be a prime driver of economic and social growth. Tertiary education has seen major investment in the city in the last three decades, and the assets in this area give it comparative advantage over all other cities in China with the exception of Beijing. The need for close links between a well supported and growing tertiary education sector which is globally competitive, and sectors like healthcare which are key users of new ideas and research from universities is obvious.

• To focus on the quality of workers and entrepreneurs to prepare them to contribute more actively to innovation. In this sense, attention to a more student-centred, more creative educational sector is important. Shanghai produces many students each year, a large number in engineering and hard sciences. But it needs to now have more support for creative, independent thinking, and for an education that shifts from rote learning to encouraging independence and critical thinking.

- To create a culturally rich, aesthetically pleasing and efficient urban environment, supportive of high value adding economic activities and an affluent and well educated work force.[1]

The report's key words are innovation, mixed economy, and sustainability. It is in three areas in the coming decade that the focal efforts need to be made. They are intimately linked to each other. The creation of a mixed economy in Shanghai will still see the service sector increase in importance – but there will still be a need for manufacturing in high added value areas simply because of the slowness with which financial service sector in particular grows and the relatively small numbers that it will employ. Innovation will be important, but in more diverse areas than just product creation, in order to create these robust manufacturing high-end sectors. Many process innovations will need to focus on energy and resource efficiency, in a city where there will be increasing pressure on these things. The road therefore to middle income, middle class status for Shanghai will be through a mixed economy, with a balance between non sector and state sector, large and small and medium companies, and innovations in education and social management. Shanghainese will experience not just changes in their material lifestyles, but also in the ways in which they live, and their own experience of agency and subjectivity in the city. Consumption will unleash new experiences of individuality. Economic restructuring will see social relationships change, with family structures in particular and the enabling networks around people transformed. The city will help China and the world address the vexed question of what the shape, form and content of Chinese modernity is. Through Shanghai we will know better what the future of Chinese society will be, and what specific differences it is likely to have from urbanization, and modernization elsewhere. Innovation therefore reaches into governance, into the way people structures their lives, and how they look at themselves and their belief

---

1. Shahid Yusuf; Kaoru Nabeshima. op. cit., p.146.

Conclusion

systems in the world. In Shanghai we will be able to see an era of wide creativity, and the structures within which the disruption that might come from this might work while building a stable sustainable future.

Alliances between different actors in this process are important. Large state supported companies will continue to matter, but their dynamic reliance on input from smaller companies will increase. Smaller companies will need to have links with larger ones in order to optimize the impact of their innovations and to help them reach domestic and international markets. Society in Shanghai will be pushed between defining overarching strategies to create cohesion and a sense of social unity while at the same time embracing the energy, creativity and freedoms that people feel within an environment where there is increasing liberty to be social and economic actors and to create bespoke networks around an individual's work and personal life. How people navigate between the demands of their own network and a sense of a broader society will be important. Diversity within this developing and fast changing mixed economy will increase, but so will the ways in which mediation has to occur between the contesting demands of different actors and groups. Innovation in arbitration, in social communication, and in creating a vision of the future society will be added to innovation in products and processes. Innovation will also be key to sorting out the massive challenges that currently exist on limited energy and resources. The space for innovation therefore is very wide. Innovative ways of thinking about innovation are also included.

There is also the critical relationship between the government, enterprises (state and non state) and the citizens. Here too Shanghai will be able to innovate, showing ways in which these three will be able to relate to each other and communicate with each other in new ways, mobilizing new forms of technology in order to do so. Citizens will be stakeholders dynamically in the future direction of their environment, rather than passive observers. They will be able to participate in decision making, and also be part of the innovative environment by exploring new ways to work with the companies and government agents that are around them. Innovation between the state and its relations with people and companies will be the most complex, but have the most far reaching impact. E governance, access to information about government services, and a more dynamic dialogue between government and people are all now increasingly possible through social media and the mobilisation of new communication technologies.

Shanghai's Future in the National Context

The World Bank also produced an important report on China nationally in 2030 in partnership with the National Development and Reform Commission (NDRC). This proposed six core strategic focal points over the ensuing two decades so that the country can achieve a balanced, harmonious model by 2030. The six focal areas in the report are as follows:

- Implementing structure reforms to strengthen the foundations of a market economy. This involves refining the role of government, restructuring state enterprises and nurturing the non state sector. Competition should be deepened, particularly in land, labour and financial markets and the movement of capital. 'While providing relatively fewer tangible public goods, the government will need to provide more intangible public goods and services like systems, rules and policies.'[2] Reforms of state enterprises would include introducing modern corporate governance, separating ownership from management and introducing ownership diversification. In the financial sector, there would be commercialization of the banking sector, allowing interest rates to be set by the market, and moving towards the internationalization of the country's financial sector. Deeper marketisation of labour would occur through reform of the Hukou household registration system, and marketisation of land, defining more clearly what land must stay as rural and which as urban, and what rights people have over the land they lease.

• Accelerating the pace of innovation and creating an open innovation system: This should happen not only through domestic cooperation on innovation but through Chinese state and non state firms participating in global research and development networks. Quality of research needs to be improved, through policy makers introducing measures that support the improvement of technical and cognitive skills of university graduates, and building world class research universities strongly linked to industry. The need for innovative cities will be important, with clusters of high talent, knowledge networks and learning institutions, along with diverse forms of capital to support the setting up of private firms.

• Seizing the opportunity of going green: Mixing market incentives, regulations, public investments, industrial policy and institutional development, to encourage green development and efficiency of resource usage. In particular, to encourage investments in low pollution, and energy and resource efficient industries. Here China's large market size, high investment rate

---

2. *China 2030: Building a Modern, Harmonious and Creative High-Income Society*. World Bank, Washington D.C., and Development Research Center of the State Council, Beijing, 2012, p.XV.

and growing private sector are all creating a benign environment for supporting going green.

- Expanding opportunities and promoting social security for all: This will be achieved by ensuring equal access for jobs, finance, social services and a portable form of social security. This will help in managing rising inequality, and employment, health and age related risks. In order to reverse the process of increased rural and urban differences in terms of access to jobs, public services and social protection, policies need to be strengthened in delivering more and better quality public services to rural areas, restructuring social security systems to ensure secure social security nets, and mobilizing both public and private, government and civil society groups to share responsibility in financing social services and public goods.

- Strengthening the fiscal system: Local governments need to have adequate revenues and financing to meet the costs of social welfare and administration. In particular, in order to strengthen the fiscal system, new resources will need to be found to meet rising budgetary demands, spending will need to be reallocated towards social and environmental objectives, and levels of government from national down to provincial need to have the right budgetary resources available to them and the autonomy and powers to raise these, along with adequate supervision.

- Seeking mutually beneficial relations with the world: This will be achieved by becoming a pro-active stake holder in the global economy, using multilateral organizations and frameworks. 'China's integration with the global economy served it well over the last three decades. By continuing to intensify its trade, investment and financial links with the global economy over the next two decades, China will be able to benefit from further specialization.'[3] To achieve this, it needs to

---

3. Ibid., p.XVII.

Conclusion

support a multilateral agreement on investment flows, integrate the Chinese financial system with the global one, and shaping the global governance agenda so that it can address issues like climate change, global financial stability, and more effective international aid architecture.

Within these proposed national objectives, Shanghai has an important role through the advanced nature of its income structure, the ways in which innovation works in the city, and the creation of a linked in community of expert groups, policy makers and economic actors. The 'China 2030' report seeks to articulate a vision which describes a remade and renegotiated social contract between citizens and government, and between actors within the economy. In this process, Shanghai can be a path finder, because of the way it occupies the forefront of the national domestic economy. In particular, the ways in which linkages can be created between highly specialist knowledge communities and policy makers, and the ways in which policy making must become more specialist and more rigourous all suit the city's immense investments in education. Community feeling within these knowledge groups and the ways in which they have access and expertise in disseminating their knowledge and advice are very important.

Social expectations are likely to rise as income levels do. Therefore the pressures on government to fulfill these expectations in terms of provision of welfare, public goods, a clean environment and healthcare and care for the elderly will all grow. For a city with a diverse population, and one which is expanding rapidly, this will create immense challenges for governance in particular. The ways in which these services are funded, and the seeking for efficiency, will prove critical. An alliance across society in order to fulfill the objectives of a balanced, well funded and sustainable health care, well being and social system has to be strengthened. Expectations about the role of the state in this and the provision of services by others have to be addressed. Shanghainese will need to feel that they are stakeholders in this process of building a well off society that realistically addresses their needs in ways which do not become fiscally crippling. As the World Bank report states, 'Without appropriate fiscal reforms, many of the other reform elements of the new development strategy would be difficult to move forward.'[4]

What the World Bank report does make clear is that Shanghai exists as part of an environment in which it is a major actor, but where on many issues it cannot act alone. The local and the global are inextricably linked. Shanghai's efforts therefore in the creation of an international finance centre are highly dependent on national decisions about the internationalization of the RMB, and the ways in which, as and when this happens, the international financial system receives this new change. Shanghai's creation of an innovative social welfare system must work within national systems of fiscal disbursement and the delegation of authority from central to regional and sub regional centres. Shanghai's environment and sustainability challenges and their solution are in particular linked to national and international policies. The careful definition therefore of key strategic areas in which the city is more autonomous than others will help to devise realistic policies in which it can be a path leaders, and others where it will work within the national domestic context while other regions and areas of the country might take a more active role.

Shanghai in the Global Context

As the last of the six national policy objective proposals makes clear in the section above, the international context is also important. The

---

4. Ibid.

world is becoming a complex and unpredictable place. That much at least most of us know. And the combination of complexity and uncertainty is often a volatile one, especially for policy makers in business and government who prefer their variables to be kept to a minimum and like certainty. 'Global Turning Points', a book already referred to previously by academics Mauro F Guillen and Emilio Ontiveros looks at the key global issues facing the world in 2012. They refer to some powerful statistics. In 2012, there were a billion people who were obese, but 800 million living in starvation. The world was becoming a more equal place in terms of wealth disparities between countries, but within those countries, within urban and rural groups, professional and non professional, men and women, inequality was actually growing. Growth had shifted to the emerging markets, which were net savers on their capital accounts, while developed countries maintained their high per capita levels of wealth, but were sinking deeper into debt.

As Guillen and Ontiveros make clear, turning points are not tipping points. They are moments of radical change, but they do not mean that something is happening for the better or the worse. They just indicate change. And in the 21st century, the one thing their work does make clear is that like it or not, change is going to happen to us all. So the more prepared we are for this, and the more pragmatic our responses, the better the outcomes might be.

China figures in this story because it is fundamental to most of the 'turning points' the authors discuss. 'Emerging economies have come to represent more than half of global activity,' they state at the head of their first chapter. 'They account for two thirds of foreign exchange reserves and are accumulating an additional two billion dollars every day.' Of this two billion dollars, China alone accounts for a half. The brute fact is that in the coming century, the money that emerging and developing countries like China saves will increasingly be sources of funds for developed economies. The political and economic arrangements for how this unprecedented new imbalance will be managed will be critical. We are living now in a world where, as the book states, '29 per cent of the total number of multinational firms, and 41 per cent of new foreign direct investment flows from emerging and developing economies.' In that sense, the era of the global dominance of North American, European or Japanese/South Korean companies is coming to an end. In fact, it has already ended.

In terms of sustainability, China's energy and food needs as it becomes a richer country in the coming decades will figure hugely, as will the environmental impact of its growth. While the country uses more renewable forms of energy, its current dependence on fossil fuels without a major technological breakthrough will continue to be the highest in the world. The 21st century will be the century of the city, with over half the world's population moving from the country to urban areas. China approached this particular turning point in 2010 when the national census then showed approximately half the country still lived in rural areas, and the other half in cities. The impact of this on the reconfiguration of the economy, on the demands of citizens towards government for public goods, on educational and development levels, is profound and will take many years to fully work out.

Governance is an issue that this book looks at in detail. States throughout the world are finding the challenge of governing greater. The authors refer to the riots in Britain in 2011, and the protest movements in the US since 2010. The economic crisis from 2008 dented the faith of many in the regulatory and administrative capacity of their governments. The G20 has become one of the key international forum for discussing issues of the global financial system, but there are questions about how well it can make binding decisions, and how quickly it is able to act. Debate continues about the mismatch between a world economy where emerging economies are becoming increasingly important, but where their representation on bodies like the International Monetary Fund is still too low.

Sustainability is broader than simply looking at energy or food needs.

It is underpinned by the notion that the activities of today should not detract from the rights of future generations to enjoy a stable, prosperous life. The challenge however is that in any political culture, selling the long term benefits of a course of action to the public when there are short term crises almost every week takes real leadership. President Obama in his re-inauguration speech in Washington on the 21st January 2013 talked of the need to tackle climate change. But his political opponents said he was acting irresponsibly and that human made climate change was unproven. The simple fact is that the carbon imprint of the average US citizen is twice that of someone in the EU, and three times that of someone in China. The skepticism of many Americans towards tackling climate change might lead to the terrible scenarios of rising sea levels and extreme weather conditions which will affect food supply that Guillen and Ontiveros talk of.

Added to this is a simply demographic change. The coming century will see populations age across the world. Already, in many developed countries from Europe to North East Asia, those over 60 outnumber those under 20. The impact of this on social behavior, on productivity and on the economy is hard to plot. Already, decisions about pension provision and what role the state plays versus individuals are becoming some of the hardest that politicians across the world have to look at. It surprises many, but in China the largest single budget line for the state is not education, or healthcare, but pensions.

What they don't foresee is a world in which, with all these dramatic shifts of economic energy and growth from one part of the world to the other, there will be a waning of the United States, and a replacement of it by China. Rather, they agree with Henry Kissinger that the future is going to be less straightforward, and that there will continue to be competing poles of influence and power, with a reduced US, a stronger China, India and Brazil, and the continuation of the influence of the European Union. 'During most of the twenty first century,' they state, 'India will be the biggest country in terms of population, China the largest in output, and the United States the richest among the major economies on a per capita basis.' They back this up with statements from the World Bank that in the coming decades, China will be the most important growth pole in the global economy, but not the only one. In that sense we are heading towards a multipolar, or polycentric world.

In this era, the greatest challenges that countries will meet will be ones they will be unable to solve on their own. From water security, to food, to climate change, to their economic development, like it or not, globalization will reign around them. The key areas that 'Global Turning Points' proposes to concentrate on are

- The labour market: we are entering an era of demographic change, something Shanghai is already experiencing with an ageing population, and a highly mobile one.

- Urbanization, with the creation of mega cities, and a new relationship with the land, the provision of water and other resources, and the balance between these and the rural areas that are expected to supply food.

- Inequality, with sharp differences not only between countries (in fact, as their book shows, these have been somewhat ameliorated in the last two decades by wealth creation in emerging markets like China's) but within countries, within specific regions and communities, so that these inequalities are highly visible – people can see if they are better or worse off that those immediately around them.

- The representation system and how people can feel more participation in the decisions effecting them

- The state apparatus and its ability to reform at a time of radical and fast change, and the international system of states where the needs of nations internally have to be balanced against their international role and their ability to seek allies and find held for their challenges in global rather than local solutions.

In none of these areas will change be easy. But nor can there be

Conclusion

no change. So the ways in which Shanghai contributes to China's national settlement of these issues in the coming decade, will also be a contribution to global solutions. Shanghai, in that sense, will not just be making decisions for itself and relevant to itself. It will be making decisions as a global actor.

What Do the Shanghainese Want?

The most suitable conclusion, however, might be to look at what people in Shanghai in 2013 say themselves about their hopes, fears and aspirations for the future of their city. How do they define the place where they live and what it should be like in 2020? What are the challenges? Here are some of their voices.

Voice One: Man in his late fifties, 'The challenges for 2020 are to concentrate on human capital, and to attract international personnel. It is to increase the educational levels in the city, although at the moment they are good, they need to get much better, and to continue to make the city a place where people want to come and not just visit but feel that it is a pleasant place, a place they can call home, and somewhere they like to live. Traffic management will be critical, along with the fair distribution of resources, and the ways in which the government locally can manage to serve people and give them what they want but also provide security and stability.'

Voice Two: Academic, 'By 2020, Shanghai will be rebuilt as a city. Its role as a commercial and trade centre will grow stronger, but for it to really grow to the next stage it needs to reform export and import taxes and compete in this area with Hong Kong. The service sector is critical, particularly in insurance, banking, and the building up of the International Finance Centre. But for this to really take off, the RMB needs to be internationalized, and that decision is in the hands of the central government. Even now, Shanghai's finance market is complete, although in terms of scale it is not vast. By 2020, the city will be a big finance centre, and probably a capital flow node to the outside world. The capital flows rate will almost certainly increase. The greatest challenge in the coming decade? To combine economic growth and social cohesion, because fast growth has often historically led to social contradictions and had an impact on social stability. Population increase in a country where there is an ageing demographic will provide great challenges. With this highly mobile and newly arrived population each year there will be issues of security. To preserve stable family structures within this will be critical. Policies need to be supported that allow fathers, mothers and children and the nuclear family to be with each other. Public goods will come under great pressure, with a huge balancing task between opening up social services but not placing impossible burdens on them, along with the imperative not to exclude people and be fair. Newcomers must feel included in the city, and have sentiments of belonging and being enfranchised. Perhaps accumulation points can be used to qualify for social welfare, or other systems which are easily implemented, fair and transparent. Greater flexibility needs to be introduced into the ways in which local government can raise money. The city's soft power needs to be built on as a result of the 2010 Expo, leveraging the exposure that event gave Shanghai globally.'

Voice Three: Think tank worker, 'Shanghai's internationalization in the next ten years will have an impact on the neighbouring cities of Hangzhou, Suzhou, Nanjing, creating a global megacity with a population of over 60 million. It will become an international hub, but on top of its material expansion there will be a profound social change. More foreigners will move to the city, perhaps seeing its non Chinese population rise to 25 per cent. Shanghai will be able to leverage on the good reputation of its products, and its history. The diversity of the city will be an asset here, in terms of its ethnic groups, the large Korean population already living there, and the different believe communities, from Jews to Christians to Muslims. The Shanghai people have a strong sense of identity from their history. That makes them more grounded. The key values of the city will be openness, justice, tolerance and trust.'

Voice Four: Businessman, 'In 2020, Shanghai will resemble New York. It will be a major finance centre – perhaps the key centre for the global economy. It will have the assets because of this to attract some of the most talented people in the world, and will be a highly internationalized centre. The city will regenerate much of its built historic legacy. It will not allow itself to lose as much of its historic buildings as Hong Kong. Nor will it allow places to resemble museum. Instead, they will be dynamic living centres of organic growth. They will be part of new lifestyles, a new ways of living. Other developing countries will be able to learn from what Shanghai has done. In particular, the development of the Hongqiao area around the airport will see a major regenerated region. Over 2 million people will live there, servicing the financial sector.'

Voice Five: Economist, 'Openness and internationalization are the key for the city's future. Since 2008, and the global economic crisis the international situation has not been good. Protectionism has been returning. This cannot shift the city from its objective to be an international centre in the next decade, despite the deterioration of the overall environment and the cautiousness by some involved in this process. The Chinese economy needs to be strengthened, which is why what is happening in Shanghai is nationally significant. Processing of goods is still dominant. Goods like iPhone and iPad are assembled in some plants in the city, but with no added value from locally and only a small proportion of their final value going to Chinese manufacturers. The GDP is on aggregate high, but amongst a huge population the wealth is spread unequally. For China into the future, and for Shanghai, the delivery of each increase in GDP will cost more and more in terms of labour, resources, and effort. Shanghai enterprises face a tough international environment to internationalise in. It isn't easy for them. This will be a slow process, and we shouldn't expect too much at the beginning. But it is happening, and will slowly increase, and by 2020 Shanghai enterprises will almost certainly be more globally active and known. The greatest challenge for local government is to create public broad consensus on how to internationalise, and how to go forward. The deepening of the market economy needs to happen much more, with the role of the state changed. There is no argument about the overarching objective of internationalization, the question is about how best to do it and the speed at which it needs to be done.'

Voice Six: Social scientists, 'Shanghai's population will continue to grow rapidly in the next decade. The household registration Hukou issue will remain, but it won't be a major problem. The real social problem is that older Shanghainese residents have to understand that wellbeing won't be sustainable and growth can't be achieved without continuing to attract large numbers of outsiders into the city. The low income Shanghainese still have a higher standard of living that migrant labourers. The challenge of dealing with the second generation of migrant labourers is acute. One issue is that there are still more high school positions than are needed. This needs to be reformed. Public goods and social welfare need to be opened up to newcomers more, especially healthcare. Local people need to understand the benefits that newcomers bring. All of them have jobs. Five per cent of Shanghainese are unemployed. In the next decade, the city will see an ageing population despite this, and one it has to have the infrastructure to deal with. In many ways, what unites people increasingly is not so much their origins, or even their belief or religious values, but their income. The middle income congregate together and increasingly express their interests collectively, as do lower middle income, poorer households, the wealthy and the super rich. Membership of income groups cuts across these sectors. In the future, there will be increasing numbers of single households.'

These are the voices of at least some people who live in Shanghai, as they look forward to what their city will be like in 2020. Shanghai as a city which is global, prosperous, sustainable, a centre of finance and culture, a place of dynamism embracing a huge wave of new people, where there is social cohesion and public services that meet the expectations of the population. These are huge challenges. But as one interviewee said in November 2012 in Shanghai, the challenges in 1990 when the city started this journey were also huge, and yet it made it this far. That at least gives some foundation for believing that we are right to be cautiously optimistic about where the city will get to in the coming decade.

Bibliography

China 2030: Building a Modern, Harmonious and Creative High-Income Society. The World Bank, Washington D.C. and the Development Research Center of the State Council, Beijing, 2012

Information Office of Shanghai Municipality; Shanghai Municipal Statistics Bureau. *Shanghai Basic Facts.* Shanghai Literature and Art Publishing Group, Shanghai, 2012

Organisation of Economic Development and Cooperation. 'Economic Survey of China 2005'. Paris, 2005, available at www.oecd.org

Kerry Brown. *The Rise of the Dragon: Inward and Outward Investment in the Reform Period, 1978-2007.* Chandos Publishing, Oxford, 2008

Edward Denison; Guang Yu Ren. *Building Shanghai: The Story of China's Gateway.* Wiley Academy, Singapore, 2006

Douglas J. Elliott. *Building a Global Financial Center in Shanghai: Observations from Other Centers.* John L. Thornton China Center, Brookings, June 2011

Andrew David Field. *Shanghai's Dancing World: Cabaret, Culture and Urban Politics 1919-1954.* The Chinese University Press, Hong Kong, 2010

Rosemary Foot; Andrew Walter. *China, the United States and the Global Order.* Cambridge University

Press, Cambridge, 2011

Peter Gallagher; Patrick Low; Andrew L. Stoler. *Managing the Challenges of WTO Participation: 45 Case Studies*. Cambridge University Press, Cambridge, 2005

Stephen Green. *China's Stockmarket: A Guide to its Progress, Players and Prospects*. The Economist/Profile Books, London, 2003

Michael B. Griffiths. *Consumers and Individuals in China: Standing Out, Fitting In*. Routledge, London, 2012

Mauro F. Guillen; Emilio Ontiveros. *Global Turning Points: Understanding the Challenges for Businesses in the 21st Century*. Cambridge University Press, Cambridge, 2012

Peter Hibbard. *The Bund, Shanghai*. Odyssey Books, Hong Kong, 2007

Chris Hogg. 'Shanghai Expo is China's New Showcase to the World'. BBC website, 29 April 2010

Rem Koolhaas; Jeffrey Inaba; Sze Tsung Leong; Chuihua Judy Chung (eds). Great Leap Forward. Taschen, Cologne, 2001

Wujun Liu; Xiang Huang. *Shanghai Urban Planning*. Shanghai Century Publishing Co. Ltd., 2007

Yasheng Huang. *Capitalism with Chinese Characteristics*. Cambridge University Press, Cambridge, 2008

Michelle Dammon Loyalka. *Eating Bitterness: Stories from the Front Lines of China's Great Urban Migration*. University of California Press, Berkeley, 2012

Chunrong Liu. 'State and Social Capital Accumulation: The Politics of Neighbourhood Council System in Shanghai'. *China Public Affairs Quarterly*, Volume 2:3, p. 225 forward

Julia Lovell. *Splendidly Fantastic: Architecture and Power Games in China*. Streika Press, Amazon and IBookstores, 2012

Victor Nee; Sonja Opper. *Capitalism from Below: Markets and Institutional Change in China*. Harvard University Press, Cambridge and London, 2012

Judith Shapiro. *China's Environmental Challenges*. Polity Press, London, 2012

Ezra Vogel. *Deng Xiaoping and the Transformation of China*. The Belknap Press of Harvard University Press, Cambridge, Mass, 2011

Jeffrey N. Wasserstrom. *Global Shanghai: 1850-1910 — A History in Fragments*. Routledge, London and New York, 2009

Guang Yang. 'Shanghai's Economic Development: Its Opportunities and Challenges in the 21st Century'. Report for the Global Urban Development Metropolitan Economic Strategy, Washington, May 2002

Shahid Yusuf; Kaoru Nabeshima. *Two Dragon Heads: Contrasting Development Paths for Beijing and Shanghai*. The World Bank/ International Bank for Reconstruction and Development, Washington, 2010

Y. M. Yeung. *Shanghai: Transformation and Modernization Under China's Open Door*. The Chinese University Press, Hong Kong

Yongding Yu. 'Revisiting the Internationalization of the Yuan'. Asia Development Bank Institute Papers No. 366, July 2012

Acknowledgements

I am deeply grateful to the Information Office of Shanghai Municipality and the China International Publishing Group for their assistance, in commissioning and then researching and writing this book.

I am also grateful to Wu Tzu-Hui for her assistance in researching and writing this book, and to the people I interviewed during the field research.

In Memory of R. H. Keable (1936-2011)

图书在版编目（CIP）数据

上海 2020：英文 /（英）布朗（Brown, K.）著．
－－北京：外文出版社，2013
ISBN 978-7-119-08630-9

Ⅰ．①上… Ⅱ．①布… Ⅲ．①地方经济－经济远景－研究－上海市－2020－英文 Ⅳ．①F127.51

中国版本图书馆 CIP 数据核字（2013）第 274857 号

英文审定：王玮
责任编辑：杨春燕　刘芳念
装帧设计：小川设计
印刷监制：冯浩

上海 2020
【英】凯利·布朗　（Kerry Brown）著

©2013 外文出版社有限责任公司
出版人：　徐　步
出版发行：
外文出版社有限责任公司（中国北京百万庄大街 24 号）
邮政编码：　100037
网址：http://www.flp.com.cn
电话：008610-68996047（总编室）
　　　008610-68996189（发行部）
　　　008610-68326174（版权部）
印　刷：北京蓝空印刷厂
开　本：787mm×1092mm　1/16
印　张：17
字　数：150 千字
2013 年第 1 版　第 1 次印刷
（英）
ISBN 978-7-119-08630-9
09800（平）

版权所有　　侵权必究　　有印装问题可随时调换